Organization

MW01181445

An Info-line Collection

Info-line is a series of "how-to" reference tools; each issue is a concisely written, practical guidebook that provides in-depth coverage of a single topic vital to training and HRD job performance. *Info-line* is available by subscription and single copy purchase.

ISBN 156-286-130-1

Library of Congress Catalog Card No. 99-073605

Printed in the United States of America.

ASTD

1640 King Street
Box 1443
Alexandria, VA 22313-2043
PH 703.683.8100, FX 703.683.8103
www.astd.org

Organizational Development

An Info-line Collection

Editor
Cat Sharpe Russo

Graphic Production
Anne Morgan

Principles of
Organization Development

Issue 8812

REVISION CONSULTANT:

Rima Shaffer
Shaffer Synergistics
1303 Geranium Street, NW
Washington, DC 20012
Tel.: 202.291.9324
Fax: 202.291.4940
email: Synergistics@erols.com

A senior faculty associate at Johns Hopkins University, Rima Shaffer has authored numerous articles on team building, organizational learning, creativity, and long-range strategic planning and capacity building. She is a frequent presenter and workshop leader at national and international conferences.

Editorial Staff for 8812

Authors
Stephanie Gordon-Cady
Kathleen Ryan

Editor
Susan G. Butruille

Revised 1999

Editor
Cat Sharpe Russo

Contributing Editor
Ann Bruen

Production Design
Anne Morgan

Principles of Organization Development

What is Organization Development?

It is both sad and ironic that we have treated organizations like machines, acting as though they were dead when all this time they've been living, open systems capable of self-renewal.

—Margaret Wheatley
Leadership and the New Science

Paradoxically, the one constant in organizational life is change. Today's organizations *must* change frequently to keep up with rapid changes in the world around them and the people within them. Any change carries risk, especially if it is haphazard. That is why the keys to organization change are attention to process and focus on goals and organizational values. And that is what organization development is all about: planned change.

Organization development (OD) is the planned process of developing an organization to be more effective in accomplishing its desired goals. It is distinguished from human resource development (HRD) in that HRD focuses on the personal growth of *individuals* within organizations, while OD focuses on developing the *structures, systems, and processes* within the organization to improve organizational effectiveness.

A successful OD process can result in the following:

● effective strategic and operational plans

● team development and effectiveness

● leadership development

● adding value, quality, competitive products, or services

Change is the intentional goal. **Development**—increased capacity and potential for effectiveness—is the purpose.

Warner Burke, in *Organization Development*, points out that OD is concerned with change that will "more fully integrate individual needs with organizational goals; lead to greater organizational effectiveness through better utilization of resources, especially human resources; and provide more involvement of organization members in the decisions that directly affect them and their working conditions."

Not all change is organization development. Burke goes on to say that organization development:

● responds to an actual and perceived need for change on the part of the client

● involves the client in the planning and implementation of the change

● leads to changes in the organization's culture or systems

While no panacea, OD functions as an enabler, establishing systems or removing obstacles to increase the organization's potential for effectiveness and success in achieving its desired outcomes.

Training and OD

So, what has OD got to do with training? Plenty. Since organization development is an education-based process, it relies heavily on training to enhance the organization's awareness and knowledge required for a successful change process.

Stephen Wehrenberg points out in *Personnel Journal* that as trainers become more experienced, they begin to see that many of their organizations' problems cannot be resolved simply by training. They see problems as part of a total system—problems such as poor communication between managers and subordinates, poor quality control, and low productivity.

Once a trainer starts to take a holistic view, he or she begins to move from trainer to "problem identifier, to evaluator, to system developer, to system integrator, to problem solver." The trainer, then, needs to understand the OD process in order to position training in the total system, and to learn how training can support OD processes as well as become an OD intervention itself.

This issue of *Info-line* is written primarily for internal trainers and consultants or training managers. It gives an overview of OD: what it is, and how it works. It also suggests ways that trainers can move toward functioning more as internal OD practitioners.

A Glossary of OD Terms

The OD effort involves a partnership among those initiating the change, those affected by it, and those guiding or facilitating it. Here are the key terms that reflect this partnership.

Consultant: the internal or external person or persons contracted to assist in accomplishing the OD effort. The relationship is temporary, with an agree-upon time of completion.

Client: the person with decision-making responsibility for the consulting assignment. Usually a manager, this person authorizes the budget and other resources for the change effort. An internal OD consultant's clients are the managers with whom he or she contracts for the OD effort; rarely is the consultant's supervisor also the client.

Client system: the group of people involved in or affected by the consulting project. It may be one work group or the entire organization.

Sponsor: the person or group with influence over the client's decisions about the project, through reporting authority, funding authority, or expertise.

Scope of work: the statement that defines the nature—and the limits—of the work to be provided by the OD consultant, including such factors as the following:

- objectives or results to be achieved
- sequence of general activities involved in the effort
- timing and deadlines
- services to be provided by the consultant
- resources available and agreed-upon fees
- role and time commitment of the client
- determining when the relationship ends

Organization Development Roots

The roots of OD extend to the work done by MIT psychologist Kurt Lewin in the 1940s. Lewin and his associates' research in group dynamics and change processes led to the "sensitivity training" of the 1960s, based on the concept that feedback causes people to become more aware of their own behavior and its impact on others' behavior.

Meanwhile, in the 1940s, the Tavistock Institute in Great Britain was developing the concept of *socio-technical systems*. This concept stated that within an organization, a social subsystem (people) and a technical subsystem (machines and other technology) exist simultaneously and interdependently. One cannot look at human and technological issues separately, but must see them in terms of their impact on one another.

Also in the 1940s, Rensis Likert and others at the University of Michigan began to summarize and report the data collected from questionnaires that assessed employee attitudes toward management and company morale. The *survey-feedback* technique set the stage for current efforts at joint action planning between managers and their work teams.

Since its beginnings, OD has undergone significant shifts, creating a current climate that links OD more fully to business success. Warner Burke cites these major developments:

- a shift from *planning* change to *implementing* change

- greater understanding and use of the terms *organizational culture* and *values*

- endorsement of participative management and other methods of employee involvement

- the importance of conflict management skills

- distinctions between leadership and management

- a larger and more systemic view of organization development

In the 1980s and 1990s, physicists' theories about chaos, complexity, and open systems influenced organization development. Organizations valuing equilibrium, at any cost, were viewed as endangered. They risked becoming closed systems that failed to change, grow, thrive, or survive. These same theorists believed that organizations, open to feedback from the external and internal environments, create processes for continuous regeneration by recognizing new patterns and creating cultures that support self-organizing systems. For more information, see *Info-line* No. 9807, "Chaos and Complexity Theory."

Organization Development Values

Leonard Goodstein, in *Contemporary Organization Development* (edited by D.D. Warrick), lists five significant attitude changes on the part of workers during the 1970s, which have carried over into the present-day work environment:

1. Less acceptance of authority.

2. Less confidence in traditional institutions and political structures.

3. Less willingness to work for the sake of work.

4. Higher expectations of rewards and challenges in the work situation.

5. Higher expectations for participation in the decision-making process.

The current practice of OD reflects these attitude changes and upholds the following primary values:

● a respect for the dignity and worth of individuals as the most important resource within an organization

● a systems approach, taking into account how individuals, their work, and the organization operate as a whole

● alignment with organization and business objectives—a commitment to enhancing the organization's capacity to produce quality goods or services

For more information on systems thinking and the systems approach to decision making in the organization, refer to *Info-line* No. 9703, "Systems Thinking."

The Seven Phases of the OD Process

The organization developer works with the client to bring about change by following an iterative process, which consists of the following:

● meeting with the client to discuss the reasons for the consultation

● gathering data about the problem

● using useful models and the practitioner's knowledge about organization development to analyze the data

● reporting the results back to the client organization

● creating the desired organizational changes

As Warner Burke points out, OD practitioners refer to the seven *phases* of the OD process, rather than the seven *steps*. This is because although the process is described as a consecutive flow, frequently it is necessary to return to a previous phase to clarify new issues. The consultant and client learn and refine their efforts throughout the intervention. And in complex projects, different activities often occur in more than one phase at a time. Briefly, the seven phases are as follows:

Phase 1: Entry
Get acquainted with a potential client and discuss the client's concerns.

Phase 2: Contracting
Agree to what needs to be done, how and when it will happen, and how much it will cost.

Phase 3: Diagnosis
Conduct an assessment to determine key issues to be addressed.

Phase 4: Feedback
Summarize and discuss the assessment data with the client and others involved with the assessment.

Phase 5: Action Planning
Plan a course of action based on the assessment data and the client's chief concerns.

Phase 6: Intervention

Implement strategies that will lead to the desired outcomes.

Phase 7: Evaluation

Determine the degree of success of the interventions, identifying positive and negative aspects related to both the outcomes gained and the process used.

Entry and Contracting

The first two phases of the OD process are **Entry** and **Contracting.** Each has distinct purposes, but they may occur simultaneously. **Entry** is the initial contact and discussion between the consultant and potential client. It is usually planned. Sometimes, however, internal practitioners find that entry discussions emerge naturally out of informal conversations with their organizations' managers.

The entry process helps the consultant and potential client decide if:

- there is a mutually understood and agreed-upon need for a change effort

- there is a commitment to undertake the effort at this time

- needed resources are available

- contractor and client have the skills and authority to contract for the effort, or whether others need to be included

Information the consultant needs to know at this point includes the following:

- evolution to the status quo

- the client's involvement in the evolution

- potential risks in undertaking the effort

- the professional backgrounds and working styles of consultant and client

- the nature of the agreement, such as a contract or letter of agreement

See the Job Aid *Preparing for the Entry Meeting* at the back of this issue of *Info-line* for steps to take prior to the important entry meeting.

Contracting sets mutual expectations for the OD effort. The contract must involve the client who has the decision-making authority to see it through, and may involve the effort's sponsors. Contracting is a necessary phase for both internal and external OD practitioners because contract discussions often can bring to the surface issues that, if they remain unsettled, can disrupt and possibly destroy the OD effort at a later phase. At a minimum, the contract should include the following elements:

- the client's desired outcomes for the effort

- the scope of work

- a work plan listing the sequence of tasks, deadlines, and people involved

- the resources to be used throughout the effort

It is helpful to consider contracting in phases. Frequently, a first contract will include an organizational assessment, a feedback report, and an action plan. See *Contracting Essentials* for points to consider.

Diagnosis

The entry and contracting phases establish working relationships and ground rules. During these phases, the practitioner begins to collect preliminary data and get an initial read on the problem. The next phase involves collecting relevant information about the situation. The data collected during this phase help the organization analyze and understand the changes it faces, and serve as a basis for planning subsequent interventions.

Diagnosis can then serve as the beginning of the "unfreezing" process, as the practitioner, and those responding to questions, study the nature of the problem as well as the organization's strengths, weaknesses, core values, tacit culture, and needs.

Contracting Essentials

Many factors need to be considered in the contracting phase, including the following:

Problem/Need
- What event(s) led to the conclusion that a change effort is needed?
- What symptoms did the client choose to notice that led to this conclusion?
- What appear to be the needs of the client?

Client
- Who is involved in the start of the project?
- Could the client change as the project progresses?
- Does the client support the change effort?
- Who will be the client's liaison?

Objective(s)
- What end result(s) is the client looking for?
- What trend(s) is the client looking for?

Shared Strategy
- What is your theoretical basis for approaching the project?
- Do you have a tentative approach to problem solution?
- What values, concepts, and principles will you and the client follow?

Consultant/Client Roles and Commitment
- What are the responsibilities, tasks, authorities, accountabilities, and level of commitment on your part and that of the client?

Client System
- Who should be involved? When?
- How will the client system be kept informed about the project? What are the deadlines? Who reports?

Results Measurement
- What will indicate to the client that progress toward the objectives is being made?
- How will these indicators be measured?
- How will the progress be fed back to the client system? What are the deadlines?

Terms
- What are the cost, budget, payment schedule?
- What is the schedule for work to be performed?

Commitment
- How important is this project to the client?
- Have the client and consultant committed the needed resources?

Documenting and Reporting
- What does the client need in order to document the project?
- What report(s) will be developed? By whom?

Communication
- Does the client expect or plan any significant changes?
- How might these changes affect the assignment?
- How will you obtain access to data or people as needed?

Follow-Through and Termination
- When will the contract end?
- Under what conditions can it be terminated or delayed?
- What evaluation or debriefing steps will be taken by you or the client?

Feedback

Feedback summarizes the data found in the diagnostic phase and sets the stage for the actions that follow. Feedback focuses on such issues as:

- structure
- policies and procedures
- work assignments
- leadership styles
- management philosophy and styles
- personality differences
- information flow
- decision making
- problem solving
- organizational culture

Feedback should be delivered:

- confidentially, if promised during the diagnostic phase

- in a clear, concise, and timely manner

- with issues identified as *interpretations* or *perceptions* rather than "the truth"

- honestly and nonjudgmentally

Feedback in the form of written reports should be written clearly and concisely, being careful to separate the consultant's interpretations and the input gathered from within the organization.

Action Planning

Action planning often happens within the context of delivering and discussing the implications of the feedback. It is in this phase that the client decides on the course of action, following discussions with the consultant and sometimes staff and work groups.

The consultant then plans and describes the following:

- What will be done and when.
- Who will be involved.
- What resources are necessary.

The action plan can also include "success criteria"—a list of outcomes that will indicate whether or not the interventions have been successful. Success criteria may include such outcomes as increased sales, higher employee satisfaction, decreased absenteeism, or fewer grievances. In this phase, it is important to identify the roles and time commitments of the client or other members of the client system. At this point, the consultant often produces a scope of work, which serves as a guide throughout the intervention and evaluation phases. The consultant may use a gap analysis or force field analysis as the basis for action planning.

Intervention

In reality, every phase of the OD process is an intervention, particularly the diagnosis and feedback phases. Interventions are strategies that lead to a change in an organization's culture. They can be directed toward individuals, work groups, or the entire organization. Here are some commonly used intervention approaches.

Individual Interventions

- job redesign
- training and management development
- career development
- individual observation and feedback
- individual skill coaching
- serving as a sounding board for decisions

Interventions Between Employees

- values clarification
- conflict resolution
- norm setting
- role clarification and negotiation
- improving communication ability
- decision making and problem solving skills
- project planning and implementation

Interventions for the Entire Organization

- vision, mission, and values development
- goal setting
- organization restructure and redesign
- commitment to new programs
- commitment to new ways of managing

Many interventions have training components, which may include the following:

- technical skills training
- administrative skills training for managers
- management development training
- communication and teamwork skills

Evaluation

Evaluation of any change effort is difficult because of the complex variables and dynamics of organization development. Evaluation is essential to determine the following: whether the client's initial goals are met; whether the change is being sustained; and formal closure on the project. The evaluation plan should begin in the early phases and be carried out incrementally throughout the project. The following key questions should be addressed in planning the evaluation:

- When will evaluation occur? After key interventions? When each phase is completed? Upon completion of the entire project?

- How will baseline data be gathered?

- How will progress be measured?

- How can evaluation processes and results be built into the project itself rather than being a separate part of the project—or an afterthought?

- At what points will it be determined that anticipated benefits are worth the costs?

An honest and effective evaluation measures not only the outcome of the project but also the effectiveness of the consultant's role. Many OD professionals ask for personal feedback at several points throughout the process. For further details, see *Info-line* No. 9705, "Essentials for Evaluation."

Is There a Mandate for Change ?

How do you know what to look for when determining whether or not an organization needs a major change effort? The more "yes" answers to the following questions, the more likely the need for organizational change.

☐ Is the organization undergoing transition from one stage of growth to another?

☐ Does the organization lack direction due to inadequate structure or guidance from upper management?

☐ Is there a sense of unrealized potential?

☐ Is the organization in an "identity crisis"—lacking a clear sense of its purpose?

☐ Does the organization cling to obsolete products, services, or practices?

☐ Is it experiencing low staff morale or high turnover?

☐ Has the organization grown very quickly—past the "Mom and Pop" stage?

☐ Are there conflicts about the organization's future direction?

☐ Has the organization experienced major changes in its environment, such as a move to new facilities?

☐ Has the organization implemented new technology?

☐ Is it bogged down with inflexible rules and directives?

☐ Are there people in place who are stopping or hindering progress?

☐ Has the organization's external environment changed dramatically?

Data Collection

The role the practitioner chooses—information specialist, trainer, problem solver, counselor—as well as the culture of the organization and the nature of the problem all affect how data are gathered, analyzed, and fed back to the client. The goal or objective of data collection must be clear. It will affect the types of data collected as well as the methods of collection used. For example, the practitioner, as information specialist, may concentrate on quantitative data and benchmark practices, presenting feedback in a formal setting, complete with charts and graphs. If data are collected to determine processes, the practitioner, as process counselor, may choose to focus on qualitative data, highlighting specific behaviors around issues like communication and conflict management and presenting the feedback informally, perhaps even as the data are gathered.

In a way, data collection is an intervention itself. A practitioner's questions, and how they are asked, can spark readiness for change. Inquiries can probe people's assumptions and stimulate thought about the organization's needs. If data collection is conducted carefully, the OD practitioner can create interest and allies, as well as raise awareness rather than promote resistance and fear. The practitioner's efforts must look beyond the symptoms and target complex interrelationships, understanding that everything he or she does becomes part of the organization's history and culture. Even a brief successful intervention can have a lasting effect; so, unfortunately, can bumbling attempts at data gathering that rouse people's ire, suspicion, and cynicism.

Before gathering data, the OD practitioner must determine the type of data to gather, who to include, how to select participants, when to gather the data, and how to gather the data.

Information Sources

1. Will I involve the entire population or will I choose a sample from the population? What percentage of the total population do I need to involve to get the information I need?

2. How will the sample be chosen? Random? Homogeneous? Heterogeneous? Stratified? Unstratified?

3. What sensitivities do I need to be aware of as I make decisions about how large a sample size to include: need for reliability of respondents to represent total population; time involved; cost of conducting the data gathering (both time and money) versus the cost and risk of not devoting time and money to this task?

Types of Data Collected

The types of data collected should be suited to the situation and the people involved. They include the following:

■ *Individual Interviews*
These are conducted privately, using a preplanned series of open questions (what, when, where, how, who?) to get the interviewee talking, followed by such questions as "Can you give me an example?" and "What did you mean by…?" They can be structured or unstructured.

■ *Small Group Interviews*
These are usually conducted in selected or random groups of three to five people. Use a flipchart for notes to help respondents clarify any points and see how their input is recorded.

■ *Written Questionnaires*
These consist of a series of clearly stated questions accompanied by a simple rating scale or method of answering the questions. They can be administered in large group meetings or distributed to data sources at their work sites.

■ *Review of Existing Data*
This may include policies, work rules, sales and profit information, turnover and absenteeism rates, grievances, employee demographics, internal promotions, and structural changes.

■ *Consultant Observation and Intuition*
In this instance, the practitioner may observe a meeting to get an idea of how people work together. He or she may note who speaks to whom, how and where a team's stated

norms differ from their actual practices, and how an organization handles conflict. Or, the practitioner may observe a work process, or track the flow of paper throughout the organization.

■ Projective Drawings and Metaphors

A picture or a metaphor speaks volumes. One valuable way to collect data about impressions and values is through the use of pictures and metaphors. People providing data may be asked to draw a picture of an ideal process or outcome, or they may be asked to supply a metaphor that describes the way the organization does business or handles a process.

■ Flowcharts of Processes

People within the organization may be asked, individually, to draw flowcharts of a procedure. This technique may be especially useful when many people are involved at different points in a complex process. The practitioner and the client system can use the data to discover differing views and missing pieces of the process.

■ Process Awareness

The practitioner may find it useful to focus the clients' awareness on their environment. How do clients know when something is working well? How do they know when something is working poorly? How aware are they of the unspeakable issues in their organization? What do they believe are the costs of these unspeakable issues?

■ Benchmarking Best Practices

The OD practitioner may gather information about best practices within or outside of the organization. These best practices can then be compared with current practices. An action plan can be developed to close the gap between the current condition and the targeted practices.

For more details, see *Info-line* No. 9008, "How to Collect Data."

Using Models to Analyze Data

Kurt Lewin said that there is nothing as useful as a good theory or model. This is particularly true in the field of organization development. OD practitioners use models to help them interpret the data they have gathered and diagnose where an organization is in the change process. Models enable practitioners to make appropriate recommendations.

In *Training and Development Handbook,* Glenn Varney echoes Lewin's belief in models as useful tools for change. He says a model can:

● serve as a basis for designing a project for change, or become the framework for a proposal for change

● be used as a road map for change, guiding the manager and organization through the change process on a step-by-step basis

● serve as a reminder of the need for a systematic approach to change

● serve as a reminder that OD is a dynamic process—that none of the variables will be constant because the entire system begins to change

As an interdisciplinary field, OD draws from the behavioral sciences of organization behavior, management and business theory, psychology, sociology, education, and counseling, as well as the physical sciences. OD practitioners approach each OD assignment with an appropriate theory base, or technical model, to guide their work and to help the client understand, support, and explain the change effort. An understanding of a classic organization theory can help:

● the consultant plan his or her OD strategy

● the client understand the change cycles that are needed

● both consultant and client focus on the appropriate elements for change

OD practitioners draw from thousands of developed theories and models. The more experienced practitioners develop their own models, based on their own and others' expertise and experience. Theory bases—whether original or borrowed—are most effective when they are relevant to the situation at hand, since rarely will one theory or model work for all OD efforts. They should be expressed in words or concepts the client can understand, and be simple and easily explained.

Once the data are gathered practitioners may use any or all of the following change theories to guide analysis. Useful models include, but are not limited to, Marvin Weisbord's Six-Box Organization Model, the Gestalt Cycle of Experience, the Nadler-Tushman Congruence Model for Diagnosing Organizational Behavior, Blake and Mouton's Managerial Grid™, Hershey and Blanchard's model of situational leadership, Lawrence and Lorsch's Contingency Theory, and Hornstein and Tichy's Emergent Pragmatic Model.

This issue of *Info-line* will describe Lewin's Three-Step Procedure of Change, Albrecht's Change Response Cycle, Lewin's Force Field Analysis, Weisbord's Six-Box Organization Model, Chris Argyris's Action Science Model of Change, the Learning Organization, John Kotter's Eight-Step Change Process, and the Gestalt Approach to Organizational Consulting.

Lewin's Three-Step Procedure of Change

Lewin's model contains the following three sequential steps.

Step 1

Unfreezing: creating a willingness and ability to change current behaviors, systems, or structures that are interfering with the organization's effectiveness or goal attainment.

Action: experiential learning, training, and data feedback to assist the client in bridging the gap between "Where or what are we now?" and "Where or what would we like to be?"

Step 2

Movement: action to move from the current situation to a new level.

Action: interventions in the client system at the individual, group, and organization levels.

Step 3

Refreezing: developing and sustaining new ways of operating and behaving that move the organization to its desired goals.

Action: training in new systems—new ways to interact, solve problems, and work with others.

Albrecht's Change Response Cycle

As the organization undergoes the change cycle just described, individuals within the organizations also experience a personal Change Response Cycle. This cycle, documented by Karl Albrecht in *Organization Development,* applies particularly when management or internal or external forces impose or dictate the change.

The Change Response includes these progressive psychological phases:

Threat: the fear of leaving the status quo, often based either on a fear of the unknown future, or a perception that the future holds equal or worse difficulties than the status quo.

Problem: the new difficulties created by the change, which must be overcome to get the job done, including the loss of clear rules and norms.

Solution: overcoming the difficulties with the new order as it becomes more routine, comfortable, and accepted for its benefits.

Habit: the new order becomes stabilized and integrated into the organization as the old procedures or operations are forgotten.

Members of the changed organization will experience this four-phase cycle more or less severely, depending on how the change is managed. OD practitioners pay close attention to the people affected by change and work to reach the Solution and Habit phases as quickly as possible.

Lewin's Force Field Analysis

Force field analysis identifies forces that sustain the status quo and helps clarify approaches needed to facilitate change. Forces may be policies, traditions, beliefs, norms of behavior, people, political or economic conditions, technology, or other factors that play a positive or negative role in the OD effort.

Kurt Lewin identified the positive change forces as "driving forces," and the negative ones as "resisting forces" that maintain the status quo. Once the driving and resisting forces are identified, the consultant and client system determine ways to eliminate or weaken the resisting forces and strengthen or add driving forces. Lewin believed it is often easier and more productive to strengthen the driving forces.

LEWIN'S FORCE FIELD ANALYSIS

"Force Field" of Driving Forces and Resisting Forces

Weisbord's Six-Box Organization Model

Marvin Weisbord developed a widely known organization model that has become a classic in the field of OD. His Six-Box Model looks at these interrelated elements within an organization.

Purposes of the organization and the members' degree of understanding, agreement, and commitment to them.

Structure, including the organizational chart, reporting relationships, job responsibilities, and delegation of authority.

Relationships among the people in the organization—their degree of interdependence, norms of behavior, conflict management, and information flow.

Rewards for doing the right things right.

Leadership style, distribution, integrity, and goal directedness.

Helping mechanisms—the varied formal procedures, informal adaptations, and management systems that help coordinate and monitor the organization's work.

Argyris' Action Science Model of Change

Chris Argyris contributed the practice of action science to organization change. In the book *Action Science,* co-authored with Robert Putnam and Diana Smith, Argyris suggests that organizations change when the people in them are committed to free and informed choice, the exchange of valid information, and internal ownership or commitment to the alternative action or choice. Individuals and organizations are encouraged to analyze their actions to discover where their behaviors lack congruence with their stated beliefs and to explore how their cognitive assumptions lead to unintended consequences.

The Learning Organization

In his book *The Fifth Discipline,* Peter Senge suggests that in a world where change is a constant, organizations are better able to carry out their missions by following the art and practices of a learning organization. The OD practitioner helps people within the organization develop these skills.

■ *Personal Mastery*
The practitioner works with employees to help them formulate individual goals, aligned with the organization's mission, and develop accountability for achieving those goals rather than scaling them back at the first sign of adversity. The practitioner

works with the organization to develop systems that support individuals in attaining mastery of both their personal and organizational goals.

■ Systems Thinking

The practitioner helps people in the organization view the total system and identify the optimum places within the system to apply leverage for change.

■ Mental Models

Like Chris Argyris, Peter Senge believes organizations can change when people identify the mental models they have constructed. By systematically probing their assumptions, people can discover how their thinking interferes with their desired outcomes. A shift in one's thinking often leads to changes in the way an organization can respond to change.

■ Building a Shared Vision

Organizations weather change by having a clear vision and mission that all employees share and support through their actions. The practitioner may help the organization create a shared vision and reach a common understanding of how each person is empowered to carry out this vision.

■ Team Learning

Organizations can create a climate for continuous change by creating a climate for continuous learning. In organizational cultures where finger-pointing and blame exist, the common response is defensiveness. Workers in these organizations learn how to shift blame to others. In cultures emphasizing team learning, team members view mistakes as an opportunity to learn and improve systems. The practitioner works to create a climate where team learning thrives and team members constantly improve processes and systems.

For more information, please refer to *Info-line* No. 9602 "16 Steps to Becoming a Learning Organization."

John Kotter's Eight-Step Change Process

In his book *Leading Change,* John Kotter describes an eight-step change process.

1. Establish a sense of urgency.

2. Create a guiding coalition.

3. Develop a vision or strategy.

4. Communicate the change vision.

5. Empower broad-based action.

6. Generate short-term wins.

7. Consolidate gains and produce more changes.

8. Anchor new approaches in the culture.

Like the other models, Kotter's guidelines can serve both as a diagnostic tool and as a map for implementing organization change.

Gestalt Approach to Organizational Consulting

The Gestalt approach to organization consulting is based on the work of psychologist Fritz Perls. In his book *Organizational Consulting: A Gestalt Approach,* Edwin Nevis states that the two main roles of the Gestalt organization practitioners are "1. To teach the client system about the Gestalt cycle of experience; and 2. To help the system improve its functioning by providing a presence that is otherwise lacking." The Gestalt cycle of experience consists of five distinct phases.

Phase 1: Awareness
During this phase, group members focus their awareness on different stimuli. In an organization, the awareness stage may begin as people gather information and data. This information and data may be gathered informally as the practitioner creates a climate where members become aware of the data that is important to them.

Phase 2: Energy/Action
During this phase, members begin to drum up interest and enrollment for their ideas.

Phase 3: Contact
In this phase of the cycle, members may come up with common objectives, a shared definition of the problem, and begin to choose a course of action.

Phase 4: Resolution/Closure
During this phase, the group reviews what has occurred, what was accomplished, and pinpoints what has been learned. The group may develop plans of action at this point.

Phase 5: Withdrawal
In the final phase, group members take time to reflect and to transition to other problems or tasks so the cycle can begin anew.

OD Roles

The consultant's role changes with each project as well as within the phases of a project. Gordon and Ronald Lippitt (in *The Consulting Process in Action*) were among the first to describe consulting roles on a continuum of directive-nondirective behavior, and to identify the need for the consultant to move in and out of these roles as appropriate for each situation.

As the consultant's role changes, so does that of the client. When the consultant is in the most directive role—that of the expert—the client has the lesser amount of control. When the consultant performs simply as a nondirective observer or reflector of the organization or client system, the client has high control and decision-making authority. As described by the Lippitts, here are some possible consultant roles, listed in order from *directive* to *nondirective.*

Technical or process expert: proposes and guides the change effort in content or process. Client relies on the consultant's expertise.

Information specialist: uses special knowledge and experience to define the problems and objectives for change.

Trainer/educator: designs, leads, and evaluates learning experiences within the change effort.

Joint problem solver: offers and helps select alternative actions needed to create desired change.

Case Study

A service industry was experiencing high levels of customer and employee dissatisfaction. Customers complained of long waits for service and personnel who seemed indifferent to their questions and their needs. Consumer groups consistently rated the facility as a poor provider of service. Employees suffered loss of morale. At every level of the organization, people blamed others for the problems.

The practitioner provided training in customer satisfaction by combining a Gestalt approach to change with Lewin's force field analysis and several of the successful practices used in learning organizations, helping the organization to do the following:

Convert resistance into willingness to experiment. The practitioner held focus groups to determine what would have to occur so employees would feel that change efforts were worth their time. This question helped engage employees in the data-gathering process, as they identified key values that needed to be addressed.

Create a shared mission, vision, and core values. Following the focus groups, the top leaders met to develop a vision and mission statement, incorporating the key values identified by employees.

Examine mental models. The entire organization met in teams to examine key beliefs that prevented employees from providing good customer service.

Create a whole systems solution to the problem. Force field analysis identified change drivers and blockers that would affect implementation of the vision. A steering committee, from the whole organization, was formed to examine and coordinate change throughout the system.

Create opportunities for team learning. Learning teams met biweekly to identify specific ways of working that helped them meet their goals and to develop plans for enhancing performance based upon the lessons learned.

Identifier of alternatives: identifies and assesses potential alternatives.

Linker of resources: identifies and retrieves useful resources (in-house and outside) to help in a particular change effort.

Fact finder: gathers, synthesizes, and analyzes data relevant to the change effort.

Process counselor: observes, diagnoses, and facilitates the human dynamics and interpersonal relationships within the client system.

Objective observer/reflector: probes, observes, mirrors, and reports what is observed; retreats from active role in client decision making.

Ethics and Other Issues

While the OD process always has a few surprises, some issues show up consistently, and some have time-honored solutions.

Confidentiality

The issue of confidentiality usually comes up in these contexts: when interacting with individuals during the assessment phase, interacting with a client throughout a project, or maintaining confidentiality after completion of a project. Confidentiality can be a tricky issue, but the solution is simple: Promises of confidentiality should be carefully considered and scrupulously followed when made.

Working Alone or With Others

Working alone with one client is often appropriate, especially when dealing with highly sensitive issues. Frequently, however, a team approach is effective. Different teaming combinations include the following:

- internal and external consultant

- internal training staff and external OD consultant teams—may be especially appropriate when handling the organizational issues involved with training programs

- two or more external consultants working with one client—particularly appropriate in complex situations where a variety of skills and perspectives are needed

- an advisory committee—composed of three to seven members representing a cross-section of people involved in the project

Politics

Because of an OD practitioner's access to confidential information, he or she often is perceived as a powerful person. A savvy practitioner avoids political alliances, strives for the middle ground, and maintains philosophical independence.

Truth or Perception?

By gathering perceptions without judging their truth or falsehood, the practitioner begins to see a more complete picture of the issues within a client system, recognizing themes and patterns essential to providing effective feedback to the client. When giving feedback, practiced consultants are careful to state their opinions as perceptions rather than as truths.

Speaking the Unspeakable

One valuable role a practitioner can perform is voicing the "unspeakable." Often organizations fail to change because members fail to recognize their "unspeakable" issues. The practitioner can give voice to issues that are difficult for the group to raise. For example: "The majority of the team members seem to have a tacit norm of starting meetings 10 to 15 minutes later than the scheduled time. Several members routinely arrive on time; most arrive late. How does the team want to handle this situation?" The practitioner may establish a contract to surface the unspeakable when the group "dances around an issue."

From Training to OD

Anyone conducting training—either internally or externally—is probably already doing some OD, or parts of the OD process, without calling it that. Training can serve as both an OD data-gathering process and as an OD intervention. Interacting with training participants during a needs assessment or in actual classroom sessions often provides the practitioner with organization data about problems and perceptions.

Thus, training serves as a diagnostic tool for the trainer, who then faces the dilemma: "Do I take this information farther, or do I finish the job and forget it?" At this point, the trainer can look upon the dilemma as an opportunity to take the first step of the OD process: the entry meeting.

There are many skills you can develop and things you can do to prepare to move from training to an OD role within your organization. Here are just a few.

- Attend OD conferences, workshops, or classes.

- Join OD organizations for networking.

- Get on OD mailing lists and listservs.

- Read the Addison-Wesley Publishing series on OD. This series of small, readable books is a primary resource for OD practitioners.

- Begin using "entry" and "contracting" to familiarize yourself with the process.

- Continually work the first few OD efforts into the training context. This will assure your client organization that you have not forgotten your original assignment as trainer and that you are merely extending that role to be more effective, Later, projects may develop without a major training component.

- Grow with the OD field.

Are You Meant to Do OD?

If you can answer "yes" to most of these questions, you probably have what it takes to be an OD consultant. Can you . . .

☐ Handle conflict—disagree, confront, reveal feelings, build trust by being clear and direct?

☐ See yourself in the various OD roles?

☐ Be objective—refrain from judging clients, understand and validate others, suspend judgment?

☐ Stay relatively detached—avoid getting hooked into others' emotions and perceptions, and maintain perspective?

☐ Give others credit—accept success without applause?

☐ Start where the client is—not where *you* wish to be?

☐ Move in and out of the "expert" role as needed?

☐ Facilitate independence in the client—be willing to be dispensable and let go?

☐ Avoid trying to do it all—refuse assignments when appropriate and reveal your limitations openly and without apology?

☐ Confront the client, tell the truth, and risk losing the assignment?

☐ Be flexible and shift direction when situations change?

☐ Keep an optimistic bias—see organizations and people as "emerging" toward their potential, not hopeless cases?

☐ Ask for and receive direct feedback?

☐ Work with people you don't like?

☐ Establish partnerships with other consultants, share expertise and support, help them look good?

☐ Use your skills for your own self-development?

References & Resources

Articles

Blake, Robert R. "Memories of HRD." *Training & Development,* March 1995, pp. 22-28.

Brache, Alan P., and Geary A. Rummler. "Managing an Organization as a System." *Training,* February 1997, pp. 68-74.

Burke, W. Warner. "The New Agenda for Organization Development." *Organizational Dynamics,* Summer 1997, pp. 6-20.

Byrnes, Jonathan L.S., and Copacino, William C. "Develop a Powerful Learning Organization." *Transportation & Distribution,* October 1990, pp. 22-25.

Church, Allan H., Janine Waclawski, and W. Warner Burke. "OD Practitioners as Facilitators of Change: An Analysis of Survey Results." *Group & Organization Management,* March 1996, pp. 22-66.

Eubanks, James L., Julie B. Marshall, and Michael P. O'Driscoll. "A Competency Model for OD Practitioners." *Training & Development Journal,* November 1990, pp. 85-90.

Garcia, Joseph E., and Carla Haggith. "OD Interventions that Work." *Personnel Administrator,* June 1989, pp. 90-94.

Hanpachern, Chutima, George Morgan, and Orlanda Griego. "An Extension of the Theory of Margin: A Framework for Assessing Readiness for Change." *Human Resource Development Quarterly,* Winter 1998, pp. 339-350.

Head, Thomas C., and Peter J. Sorensen Jr. "Critical Contingencies for the Evaluation of OD Interventions." *Organization Development Journal,* Summer 1990, pp. 58-63.

Katz, Judith H., and Robert J. Marshak. "Reinventing Organization Development Theory and Practice." *Organization Development Journal,* Spring 1996, pp. 40-47.

Liang, Chaucer Chaoyun, and Thomas M. Schwen. "Critical Reflections on Instructional Design in the Corporate World." *Performance Improvement,* September 1997, pp. 18-19.

McVinney, Chuck. "Dream Weaver." *Training & Development,* April 1999, pp. 38-42.

Peters, Diane McFerrin. "Dare to Care as Fiercely as You Compete." *Journal for Quality and Participation,* January/February 1999, pp. 20-23.

Raimy, Eric. "Precious Moments." *Human Resource Executive,* August 1998, pp. 26-29.

Wah, Louisa. "Welcome to the Edge." *Management Review,* November 1998, pp. 24-29.

Wehrenberg, Stephen B. "The Vicious Circle of Training and Organizational Development." *Personnel Journal,* July 1986, pp. 94-100.

Books

Albrecht, Karl. *Organization Development: A Total Systems Approach to Positive Change in Any Business Organization.* Englewood Cliffs, NJ: Prentice-Hall, 1983 (out of print).

Beckhard, Richard, and Wendy Pritchard. *Changing the Essence.* San Francisco: Jossey-Bass, 1992.

Bellman, Geoffrey M. *The Consultant's Calling.* San Francisco: Jossey-Bass, 1990.

Block, Peter. *Flawless Consulting.* San Diego: University Associates, 1981.

Bolman, Lee G., and Terrence E. Deal. *Reframing Organizations.* San Francisco: Jossey-Bass, 1997.

Burke, W. Warner. *Organization Development.* Reading, MA: Addison-Wesley, 1987.

Chawla, Sarita, and John Renesch. (eds.). *Learning Organizations.* Portland, OR: Productivity Press, 1995.

Cloke, Kenneth, and Joan Goldsmith. *Thank God It's Monday!* Chicago: Irwin Professional Publishing, 1997.

DiBella, Anthony J., and Edwin C. Nevis. *How Organizations Learn.* San Francisco: Jossey-Bass, 1998.

Kotter, John P. *Leading Change.* Boston: Harvard Business School Press, 1996.

References & Resources

Info-lines

Lippitt, Gordon L., and Ronald Lippitt. *The Consulting Process in Action.* San Francisco: Pfeiffer, 1986.

Maurer, Rick. *Beyond the Wall of Resistance.* Austin, TX: Bard Books, 1996.

Mink, Oscar G., James M. Shultz, and Barbara P. Mink. *Developing and Managing Open Organizations.* (2nd edition). San Francisco: Pfeiffer, 1991.

Morgan, Gareth. *Creative Organization Theory.* Thousand Oaks, CA: Sage Publications, 1989.

———. *Images of Organization: The Executive Edition.* San Francisco: Berrett-Koehler, 1998.

Nevis, Edwin C. *Organizational Consulting: A Gestalt Approach.* Cleveland: Gestalt Institute of Cleveland Press, 1987.

O'Toole, James. *Leading Change.* San Francisco: Jossey-Bass, 1995.

Quinn, Robert E. *Deep Change.* San Francisco: Jossey-Bass, 1996.

Robinson, Dana G., and James C. Robinson. *Performance Consulting.* San Francisco: Berrett-Koehler, 1996.

Schein, Edgar H. *Process Consultation.* Vol 1 and Vol 2. Reading, MA: Addison-Wesley, 1988.

Senge, Peter M. *The Fifth Discipline.* New York: Doubleday, 1990.

Senge, Peter, et al. *The Fifth Discipline Fieldbook.* New York: Doubleday, 1994.

———. *The Dance of Change.* New York: Doubleday, 1999.

Varney, Glenn H. "Organization Development and Change." In *Training and Development Handbook.* (4th edition). Edited by R.L.Craig. New York: McGraw-Hill, 1996.

Warrick, D.D. (ed.). *Contemporary Organization Development.* Alexandria, VA: ASTD, 1985 (out of print).

Weisbord, Marvin. *Productive Workplaces.* San Francisco: Jossey-Bass, 1987.

Wheatley, Margaret J. *Leadership and the New Science.* San Francisco: Berrett-Koehler, 1994.

Callahan, Madelyn R. (ed.). "Be a Better Needs Analyst." No. 8502 (revised 1998).

Gilley, Jerry W. "How to Collect Data." No. 9008 (revised 1998.)

Long, Lori. "Surveys from Start to Finish." No. 8612 (revised 1998).

Marquardt, Michael. "16 Steps to Becoming a Learning Organization." No. 9602 (revised 1997).

Titcomb, T.J. "Chaos and Complexity Theory." No. 9807.

Waagen, Alice. "Essentials for Evaluation." No. 9705.

Zulauf, Carol Ann. "Systems Thinking." No. 9703.

Job Aid

Preparing for the Entry Meeting

Once a job or contract to deliver training has ended, you may see the need to sell your client or sponsor on the value of organizing the information you have gathered and using it to enhance the organization's effectiveness. Your training client or sponsor may also be your prospective OD client. If not, he or she may be willing to initiate an entry meeting for you. Here is a checklist of bases you will want covered before that important meeting.

☐ Are you sure you are going to the right person—the one who can address the issues you have heard during the training process?

☐ If the data you have gathered during the training event will surprise the client, are you at liberty to divulge the information and elaborate on it?

☐ If you cannot divulge the information, are you prepared to suggest a formal data-gathering process to confirm and provide details?

☐ If the client is not surprised to hear the information, are you prepared to ask what has already been done to address the issues?

☐ If you succeed in contracting to further the process, are you prepared to offer to do the work yourself, or to suggest calling another consultant to do the following:

- supplement your skills

- provide another viewpoint

- deliver conclusions that may be risky for you to deliver yourself

Questions for a Diagnosis Interview

Once you have prepared for the entry meeting, be clear in your mind what questions you need to ask in order to properly assess the needs of the client.

☐ What are the strengths of the organization?

☐ What aspects of the organization need to improve?

☐ What is your understanding of the organization's mission?

☐ Is it always clear to whom you are responsible and for what you are responsible?

☐ Draw an organizational chart, using solid lines to show reporting relationships, and dotted lines to show working relationships.

- Does this system lead to the best use of your resources?

- Are there any changes you would make that would strengthen the way these relationships are organized?

☐ What barriers prevent you from doing your best work?

☐ If you could make three changes that would improve any aspect of the organization, what would they be?

☐ What words or phrases would you use to describe the way in which the following are handled?

- interpersonal communication

- information flow

- conflict resolution

- decision making

Job Aid

Data Analysis Planning Guide

There are many ways the OD practitioner can analyze information and feed it back to the organization. The choice will depend on the role the practitioner takes during the consultation. The expert consultant is likely to create a written report and present it to the organization. The joint problem solver might work with an advisory committee to analyze the data and make recommendations to the organization. The process consultant might feed the data back during an observation. Regardless of the role taken, the practitioner should honor commitments made about confidentiality, analyze the data in a timely fashion, and feed it back so the client can hear it and then act upon it.

Data Presentation

1. Are the data quantitative in nature?

   - Will I discuss frequencies?

   - Will I present ranges?

   - Will I discuss central tendencies (mean, median, mode)?

   - Will I analyze the variances?

   - How will I describe the sample or population?

   - Do I want to compare the data (for example, females who value team work compared with males who value team work)?

   - What does the information support?

   - What can one infer from the data?

   - What caveats must be emphasized?

2. Are the data qualitative in nature?

   - What trends do I or the client notice?

   - What models can be applied to the data?

   - What themes emerge?

   - What paradoxes do I notice? What meaning does the group give the paradoxes?

   - Can any of the data be quantified, and is it useful to do so (for example, frequency at which a certain theme appeared)?

The material appearing on this page is not covered by copyright and may be reproduced at will.

Organizational Culture

Issue 9304

Organizational Culture

CONSULTING AUTHOR:

Kenneth L. Murrell, Ph.D.
The University of West Florida
11000 University Parkway
Pensacola, FL 32514
Tel. 904.474.2310
Fax. 904.474.2314
E-mail: kmurrell@uwf.edu

Dr. Kenneth Murrell is professor and co-coordinator of the Organization Development and Leadership program at The University of West Florida and president of Empowerment Leadership Systems. He has been involved in organizational development work since the early 1970s. In addition to his work with the United Nations, he has consulted to numerous corporations: Motorola, Toyota, and BellSouth, as well as smaller companies and non-profit agencies.

Editorial Staff for 9304

Editor
Barbara Darraugh

ASTD Internal Consultants
Jan B. Throckmorton
Michele Brock

Revised 1997

Editor
Cat Sharpe

ASTD Internal Consultant
Ethan Sanders

Reprinted 1999

Culture Defined

Definitions of corporate culture range from the simple statement, "that's the way we do things around here" to the more elaborate explication, "shared meanings that govern the nature of labor-management relations, the types of people hired, performance and promotion criteria, rewards and censure, work climate, and management style." A more complete, yet straight forward definition is offered by the U.S. Government Accounting Office, "culture is the underlying assumptions, beliefs, attitudes, and expectations shared by an organization."

By understanding organizational culture, its symbols and hidden meanings, its values, and its underlying assumptions, managers can change—or at least manipulate—culture, and in so doing, change the behavior of individual workers. Rosabeth Moss Kanter, author of *The Change Masters: Innovation and Entrepreneurship in the American Corporation*, writes:

"Culture manifests itself through numerous organizational structures; it is made concrete by organizational events. And, thus, it can be managed; it can be shifted by changing concrete aspects of an organization's functioning. For example, values do not exist independently of rewards; preferences do not exist independently of political signals from power holders; expectations about activities do not exist independently of action vehicles or programs permitting the activities."

Training has a specific and unique role in the maintenance or manipulation of culture: Many corporate values and beliefs are disseminated through training programs, through orientation programs, and systems where new employees are "socialized"—first introduced to the organization's culture. According to author Peter S. DeLisi, "shifts in the larger culture influence individuals, who in turn influence organizational culture, which in turn affects organizational structure."

Essentially, an organization's culture helps define the following:

- corporate strategy

- the organization's response to crises

- its relationships with customers, employees, shareholders, government agencies, media, and the community

- who it will hire and how employees will be trained

- management style

- what constitutes successful and unsuccessful performance

- behaviors that will be disciplined

- workplace climate

Culture Counts

In the book *Built to Last,* authors James Collins and Jerry Porras use the example of Merck & Co., Inc., a pharmaceutical company that is "in the business of preserving and improving human life," and how it applied its core ideology after discovering and developing a cure for "river blindness" in 1982. The disease is carried by parasitic worms that invade the body tissue and previously infected over a million people in the Third World, causing blindness. Merck not only developed Mectizan, the drug to cure this disease, but when the company could not find a customer base with enough purchasing power to buy the drug, Merck decided to freely dispense Mectizan to all those individuals who required it.

When asked in 1991 why his company provided Mectizan at no charge, Merck's then CEO, P. Roy Vagelos, said that his scientists would have been "demoralized" if Merck had not distributed the drug, because the scientists truly believed they were "in the business of preserving and improving human life."

These same ideals—Merck's organizational cultures—have defined the company since the late 1920s. In the words of George Merck II, who took over from his father in 1925, "Here is how it sums up: We try to remember that medicine is for the patient. We try never to forget that medicine is for the people. It is not for the profits. The profits follow, and if we have remembered that, they have never failed to appear. The better we have remembered it, the larger they have been."

The story of Merck and Mectizan shows how the culture of an organization can have far-reaching effects on everyday life in the workplace, decision making, and crisis management. This *Info-line* will discuss cultures in organizations, how they are developed and managed, and will also provide tips on how to better understand the culture of your own organization.

Cultural Concepts

People usually dislike uncertainty and randomness. We try to find meaning in chaos and establish order in everyday activities and events. The establishment of cultures provides us with common ideas that help us cope—both individually and as a group—with life's ambiguities.

According to Harrison Trice and Janice Beyer, authors of *The Cultures of Work Organizations*, established cultures share the following six major characteristics:

■ *Collectiveness*
Cultures reflect the commonly held beliefs of their members. Those who fail to endorse and practice the prevailing beliefs, values, and norms of a culture are marginalized and may be punished or expelled.

■ *Emotionally Charged*
Because cultures evolve to help deal with anxiety, they are infused with both emotion and meaning. "People cherish and cling to established ideologies because they seem to make the future predictable by making it conform to the past," Trice and Beyer note.

■ *Historically Based*
A specific culture results from the unique history of a particular group that is coping with a special set of physical, social, political, and economic circumstances. "Cultures cannot be divorced from their histories and they do not arise overnight," they stress.

■ *Inherently Symbolic*
Symbolism—things representing other things— plays an important role in cultures. Symbols are the "most general and pervasive of cultural forms," Trice and Beyer say.

■ *Dynamic*
Cultures, although they're passed from generation to generation and create continuity, are constantly changing.

■ *Vagueness*
Cultures "incorporate contradictions, ambiguities, paradoxes, and just plain confusion," Trice and Beyer assert. Cultures may have both central and peripheral elements. Fuzziness marks the peripheries and may represent miscommunications, influence from sub- and countercultures, or changing circumstances.

Does your organization's culture promote high performance? See how it scores on the Organizational Indicators Test on the next page to find out.

Substance and Form

Cultures have both substance and form: Substance is the ideology—the shared systems of beliefs, values, and norms—represented. Form is the way that individual members of a culture express themselves. While form may be readily apparent in a culture, often the substance of a culture must be inferred.

Substance

The substance of an organization's culture reflects many beliefs, only some of which originate within the organization. Organizations reflect transnational, national, industrial, and occupational ideologies.

Transnational ideologies transcend national boundaries, according to Trice and Beyer, who list science, capitalism, and Protestantism as transnational cultures. Of these, the most pervasive is science. All nations, they contend, seem to be "relatively united in their belief in the value and efficacies of science." Environmental concerns, the dangers of nuclear energy, the threatened extinction of wildlife, and world hunger are four issues "that have stimulated transnational movements and ideologies," they add.

National ideologies reflect beliefs about work and doing business that transcend differences among industries and specific companies. Dutch professor Geert Hofstede outlined four basic "dimensions" of national cultures based on survey data from 160,000 IBM managers in over 40 countries. The four dimensions are as follows:

Organizational Indicators Test

Frederick E. Schuster, a management professor at Florida Atlantic University developed the following 20 questions to provide some quick insight into whether your organization's culture promotes high performance. See page 39 for scoring details.

1. Could you describe your organization's culture in one to three sentences? ☐ Yes ☐ Unsure ☐ No

2. Could most employees in your organization? ☐ Yes ☐ Unsure ☐ No

3. Does your organization give as much attention and respect to employees as to its *best* customer? ☐ Yes ☐ Unsure ☐ No

4. Do employees have confidence that the organization will treat them fairly in all situations, regardless of the circumstances and pressures? ☐ Yes ☐ Unsure ☐ No

5. Are employees intensely proud of the product or service which they produce, and of the organization they work for? ☐ Yes ☐ Unsure ☐ No

6. Does your organization make use of an *annual* climate survey or opinion survey to regularly and routinely obtain feedback on employees' perceptions? ☐ Yes ☐ Unsure ☐ No

7. Is this data given serious attention and really acted on? ☐ Yes ☐ Unsure ☐ No

8. Does your organization undertake major efforts to keep employees fully and accurately informed about everything going on (future plans, changes, decisions being made, and so forth) whether they "need to know" or not? ☐ Yes ☐ Unsure ☐ No

9. Do employees assume they will *always* hear any news first through organizational channels—not the newspaper, TV, radio, or "grapevine"? ☐ Yes ☐ Unsure ☐ No

10. Is widespread participation of rank-and-file employees in important management decisions actively encouraged? ☐ Yes ☐ Unsure ☐ No

11. Do employees perceive a close tie between performance and rewards—that top performers get significantly greater rewards than average performers? ☐ Yes ☐ Unsure ☐ No

12. Do rank-and-file employees have any choice or control over the form in which they receive their compensation (through such programs as flexible compensation and benefits)? ☐ Yes ☐ Unsure ☐ No

13. Does your organization have a productivity bonus plan that allows groups or individuals to share directly in the financial benefits from higher productivity? ☐ Yes ☐ Unsure ☐ No

14. Is the performance of executives in managing people actually measured in some rational way and is this evaluation given equal weight along with other factors such as unit profitability in determining executive salary and bonuses? ☐ Yes ☐ Unsure ☐ No

15. Does the organization avoid the use of divisive status symbols, such as executive dining rooms, reserved parking spaces, and elaborate offices at a great distance from operations? ☐ Yes ☐ Unsure ☐ No

16. Is *everybody* on a first-name-only basis? ☐ Yes ☐ Unsure ☐ No

17. Does the organization encourage participative management by actively seeking the ideas and suggestions of *all* employees? ☐ Yes ☐ Unsure ☐ No

18. Are employees paid fairly and adequately in relation to what other employers are paying for similar work? ☐ Yes ☐ Unsure ☐ No

19. Do employees widely perceive that their jobs provide opportunity for growth, development, and advancement? ☐ Yes ☐ Unsure ☐ No

20. Do employees in the organization widely perceive that effective performers are guaranteed permanent jobs? ☐ Yes ☐ Unsure ☐ No

1. Individualism/collectivism. Individualism is the level of personal choice in the job and self-reliance. Collectivism is social cohesion and reflects the workers' expectations that the employer will care for them and provide security. Most Americans, Europeans, and Australians value individualism; Japanese, Pakistani, Greek, and Turkish workers rate high in collectivism.

2. Power/distance. This is the extent to which power is concentrated or dispersed through the organization and the extent to which less powerful individuals accept the power distribution. "High-power distance" is a situation in which employees have little involvement in making decisions; "low-power distance" reflects more participative management. Countries where high power distance prevails include India, Indonesia, and the Philippines; low power distance prevails in Sweden, Austria, and Israel.

3. Uncertainty avoidance. This dimension measures people's tolerance for uncertainty and the extent to which individuals try to avoid uncertainty by working for organizations that provide career stability. Japan, Portugal, and Greece have high uncertainty avoidance cultures, while Singapore, Denmark, and the United States rate low in uncertainty avoidance.

4. Masculinity/femininity. Masculinity is the extent to which assertiveness and dominance of others is approved; femininity is the emphasis on caring and nurturing. Japan, Great Britain, and Ireland reflect the masculine side, while Israel, Denmark, Sweden, and Thailand lean toward the feminine.

Industrial ideologies are business conditions such as competitiveness, historical development, dominant technologies, and customer requirements that help shape an organization's beliefs and values. These shared values are apparent in every industry.

Occupational ideologies are formed by professions represented within an organization that may have their own cultures. Professionals often receive their training and indoctrination prior to employment by a particular organization. Their loyalty, therefore, may be to the profession rather than to the employing organization. They are represented by a specific code of ethics, common and sometimes exclusionary language, and membership in a professional organization.

Forms

While the substance of a culture is the base or fundamental element of that culture, form is the visible expression of the substance. "Forms condense and make cultural ideologies concrete," Trice and Beyer note. "They serve as sense-making mechanisms by which members of a culture can either consciously or unconsciously derive meaning from their situation." See "More Management Models" on the next page to find your management's model or style.

Trice and Beyer have categorized cultural forms into the following five categories:

■ *Symbols*
Signs, logos, pictures, insignias, uniforms, workplace layout—anything that can represent something or someone else is a symbol. Uniforms, for example, are symbols because they represent the idea that the person in the uniform will conform to the organization's norms. Open floor plans physically represent an organization's egalitarian philosophy, while corner offices connote high status. Symbols are "multivocal" in that they can carry more than one meaning.

■ *Management Style*
The style of managing work relationships generally is mandated by the organization's culture. This concept is important because it allows workers to generate a philosophy that gives meaning to their work, which in turn generates commitment and serves as an informal control on behavior. "A management style will evolve," Graham Prentice, a personnel manager at Nestlé, writes, "within the prevailing set of values and beliefs held by an organization." Prentice cites Roger Harrison's four cultural management types, which he included in an article for the *Harvard Business Review:*

Power orientation, which is frequently found in smaller, entrepreneurial businesses.

More Management Models

Management styles have been categorized and explained by many business professors and sociologists. The different models often overlap. In addition to the substance and form models discussed in the text what follows may be also useful in determining your corporate culture.

Model A

Carol Hymowitz outlined four types in *The Wall Street Journal.*

■ *Academies*
Organizations that move new hires through a series of training programs and jobs. As discussed on page 12, Disney requires all of it new hires to attend Disney University where orientation and internal socialization and training is taught by its own instructors and where the personnel office is referred to as "casting."

■ *Fortresses*
Organizations that are struggling to survive and can't offer job security. They offer the excitement of a "turn-around" effort and a sense of individual contribution to the firm's success.

■ *Clubs*
Organizations that have no fast track; all managers are expected to work their way up. They are characterized by loyalty, fitting in with the group, and getting to know the right people.

■ *Baseball teams*
Organizations that place high value on performance and talent, entrepreneurial skills, and offer large financial rewards and recognition. "Baseball teams" are common in advertising, software development, and consulting.

Adapted from "Which Corporate Culture Fits You?" The Wall Street Journal, July 17, 1989. All Rights Reserved.

Model B

Robert Poupart and Brian Hobby list five more traditional management models:

■ *Father-founder*
Organizations in this mode usually have a strong leader—"The Boss." Career development, promotions, pay, work hours, and other systems are dependent on his or her whim. These organizations are characterized by informality, flexibility, adaptability, and strong commitments.

■ *Bureaucracies*
Organizations geared toward cost efficiency and respect for proper procedures. Systems are highly procedural, roles are specifically defined, and work is predictable. Individual career paths are highly formalized and channeled through job postings.

■ *Participative*
Organizations value cohesion and loyalty to the group. Productivity is measured by member commitment, involvement, and motivation. Careers focus on job enrichment and enlargement, and avoid career "paths" as being legalistic. Self-determination and autonomy rule.

■ *Professional*
Professional organizations are based on expertise. Members of these cultures identify with the occupation, rather than the employing organization. Professional organizations disdain hierarchies. Career advancement is based on increasing expertise.

■ *Managerial-entrepreneurial*
These organizations concentrate on the customer or client. Adaptability to the customer's needs is the organization's preoccupation. "Advocates of this culture favor small, autonomous units organized as cost or product centers in a flat structure that is simple in form and employs a lean staff," Poupart and Hobby observe.

Adapted from "Changing the Corporate Culture to Ensure Success." National Productivity Review, Summer 1989. All rights reserved.

Role orientation, which is typified by a heavily proceduralized bureaucracy.

Task orientation, which emphasizes team and achievement. Individuals in this group are usually internally motivated.

Support orientation, which bonds work groups through close, warm relationships.

Although there is usually one dominant management style, each organization has a secondary style. Styles may vary by department and subculture as well.

■ *Language*

All organizations have their own language; all but the simplest have several languages. Members need to learn the lingo to carry out their work activities and interact with various subcultures. Within an organization, the most visible forms of culture often are the written artifacts that exist—mission statements, credos, ethical codes, and vision statements. The language category, however, also includes jargon and slang, metaphors, slogans, gestures, humor, and the "grapevine."

■ *Narratives*

Some beliefs and values are too complex to be encapsulated by a metaphor or slogan. These ideologies are then expressed in stories or fairy tales, legends, sagas, and myths. The differences between the levels are how much truth is in each telling.

Stories or fairy tales are usually brief, simple, and contain some embellished truth. They often involve chances for promotion, the fear of being fired, serious work obstacles, and response to mistakes. For example, *We always promote from within.* Official stories are flattering to the organization, while unofficial stories can be unflattering.

Legends are more uplifting than stories and contain elements that cannot be fully explained by ordinary, mundane circumstances. A legend, for example, might be: *During the 'official' part of a company picnic, the sun broke through the clouds when the president announced the formation of a new subsidiary. This was a good omen.*

Sagas are about heroic exploits that are usually based on truth. An example of a saga is: *I once had a supervisor who really helped a terminally ill co-worker. Because of her various doctor's appointments and her chronic illness, she had used up all of her sick leave. Her supervisor explained the situation to her staff and requested that the staff pick up the woman's routine duties. In this way, she kept the worker on the payroll for several months, before being forced by management to place the worker on sick leave.*

Myths are largely inventions and are used to explain the origins of the organization or transformations of great importance. A myth about the foundation of one publishing house is that the founder bought it with money won during his weekly poker games.

■ *Practices*

Behaviors become cultural forms, Trice and Beyer note, "when their efficacy is taken for granted and their appropriateness is rarely questioned." These practices include rituals and taboos, and rites and ceremonies.

Rituals often have negative connotations except as used in churches, fraternities, and sororities. "Oh, he or she is only going through a ritual—nothing will really come of it." Rituals can play meaningful roles, however. Historically, cultures have used ritual to create order, clarity, and predictability, especially in mysterious and complex situations. Rituals help to reduce uncertainty and anxiety and bind people together. According to authors Bolman and Deal in *Reframing Organizations*, rituals in the workplace include such activities as performance appraisals, regular committee meetings, management training programs, and hiring tests and interviews.

Taboos, on the other hand, are prohibited behaviors, such as open discussion of salaries or stock options and, frequently, one's true emotions.

Rites and ceremonies are social dramas that require preplanning and have audiences. Trice and Beyer have identified six types of rites that occur in organizations:

Rites	Examples
rites of passage	completion of orientation courses
degradation	firing
enhancement	sales meetings
renewal	annual meetings
conflict reduction	collective bargaining
integration	holiday party

Subcultures and Countercultures

Subcultures exist within all but the smallest cultures. They grow out of different occupations, workforce levels and locations, and the provision of different products and services. Subcultures may be starkly different from the central organizational culture and from each other. They fall into three main groupings:

1 Enhancing subcultures embrace the dominant culture's values even more fervently than the dominant culture does.

2. Orthogonal subcultures accept the dominant culture's values but have nonconforming sets of values they consider their own.

3. Countercultures challenge the values of the dominant culture.

Groups of individuals—both formal and informal—can form subcultures. Informal groups arise spontaneously, while formal groups are arranged by management. Informal groups include:

Friendship groups, which engage personal interests, liking, and social intimacy.

Cliques, which are friendship groups that seek power; their members "consciously use collective resources to further both individual and collective aims," Beyer and Trice note.

Cabals and coalitions, which exist to further mutual interests but are not necessarily based on friendship. A cabal is a small, temporary group with an explicit objective; a coalition is both larger and longer lived than a cabal.

Formal groups are usually determined by authority and formal structures such as:

- technology and work flows
- departments
- distinctions between line managers and staff
- distinctions between hierarchical levels

The most frequent basis for a subculture is occupation. Occupational subcultures exert influence both internally and externally around defined tasks. Occupational subcultures have distinct languages, symbols, and rites and they set and maintain criteria for the successful performance of the occupation. They may create "alternative, potentially conflicting bases of control in organizations," note Trice and Beyer.

The effects of subcultures are positive when they pull together on issues of vision, strategy, and management style. Their effects can be negative when the subcultures disagree with each other or the central culture about what is important to the conduct of business. In the case of a divisive subculture, management should try to preserve the pride, motivation, and innovation residing in the separate subcultures while building a shared vision of the whole organization. See "Handling Diversity" on the next page for tips on managing differences in the workplace.

Countercultures

Subcultures that question basic assumptions and confront the central culture in any one of a number of ways become countercultures. Edgar H. Schein, author of *A Manager's Guide to Corporate Culture* notes, "efficient countercultures both ridicule and offer alternatives to customary values and beliefs." As Trice and Beyer observe, "countercultures express the situation from which they emerge—pushing away from it, deploring its contradictions, caricaturing its weaknesses, and drawing on its neglected and underground traditions."

Handling Diversity

What happens when corporate culture meets ethnic diversity? Although corporations thrive on cultural cohesiveness—a sharing of values and goals—the increasing diversity of the workforce brings different values and goals into the workplace. Noting that "self-interest will force organizations to change," Jeffrey Goldstein and Marjorie Leopold assert that in "attracting and retaining skills, conscientious employees will become more critical than ever as well-publicized demographic changes, combined with other social and economic factors, limit the pool of qualified new hires." Goldstein is a professor at Adelphi University and Leopold is a consultant in equal employment opportunity.

Goldstein and Leopold offer the following guidelines through the cross-cultural minefield:

Don't avoid the issue of diversity. "Being treated fairly means to be treated the same as everyone else *and* recognizing how each employee is different," they say. Open discussions about ethnic differences between managers and employees and among employees themselves can be held during staff meetings or informally during routine work activities. However, managers need to be careful not to pry into their employees' personal lives.

Explore people's unique backgrounds/influences. Managers should discuss their own backgrounds as a means of encouraging their employees to open discussions about their cultural, ethnic, racial, or gender differences. Celebrating diversity through special events—honoring St. Patrick's Day or Chinese New Year's or Black History Month—will allow individuals to express their ethnic identities while encouraging awareness. However, you can't force people to participate in these activities.

Use tact and respect the individual. Emphasize similarities between cultures. It may be possible to put differences into a cultural context. For example, a manager might discuss the cultural basis of his or her way of dress with an employee who wears a kente cloth to work.

Stay within EEO guidelines. Managers shouldn't tolerate racist or sexist remarks or jokes. Emphasize the organization's equal employment opportunity guidelines when discussing diversity.

Balance personal and professional requirements. A manager's role is to link employees to the organization's values, standards, and goals. Employees need to know how they fit into the organization's culture.

Explain the unwritten rules. The organization's culture may impede an employee's individual expression. Talk about rules concerning dress, working late, acceptable language, and how to approach bosses and disagree. Explain why the rules are appropriate. Be specific.

Openly discuss the organization's culture. These discussions will ensure that the employee knows that the "company's culture isn't just your perception or biases," Goldstein and Leopold say. Co-workers, they continue, "might offer support and function as role models."

Several things are likely to produce countercultures:

■ *Mergers*
Employees of companies that are acquired by other organizations may feel that their organization is being plundered, exploited, and occupied. It may be necessary to remove the top executives of the acquired organization to eliminate possible counterculture leaders.

■ *Rebels*
Trice and Beyer say that, "rebels are determined innovators [who] feel they have to oppose the dominant culture to…achieve changes they envision." Usually, rebels at high levels are either removed or co-opted.

■ *Employee Discontents*
Countercultures may be based on strong employee grievances. These groups form around shared, severe discontents and usually last only as long as the issues that provoke them. Only management's inflexibility concerning the grievance can generate the maintenance of such a counterculture over a long period of time.

■ *Deviant Behavior*

Subcultures that engage in activities that are both counterproductive and opposed to the dominant culture have the seeds of a counterculture. Some deviant behavior, such as drinking or using illegal drugs on the job, may not generate countercultures because the activity is not intended to interfere with the organization's operation. Other deviant behaviors may arise in occupational subcultures where the subculture's ideology conflicts with the organization's.

■ *Social Movements*

Individuals who may have experienced some broadening of their opportunities may form countercultures to reach parity. Women and minority group members exemplify this type of discontent. Schein notes that "countercultures, in spite of their adversary appearance, can have certain definite advantages—as safety valves, for dissent and crucibles for new ideas."

Management and Maintenance

Culture is a tool used to define acceptable behaviors and control employees. As such, it is a management resource that can be used to meet the organization's objectives, just like knowledge, machinery, raw materials, dollars, and human resources. Before culture can be manipulated, however, management needs to know what the culture is and how it works; recognize and use the "levers" that influence culture; and be clear about whether they want to maintain, change, or establish a culture.

Much of an organization's espoused culture is apparent in its mission and policy statements, credos, and press releases. Other sources of corporate knowledge are newsletters, annual reports, corporate histories, and articles and books written by current and former executives. Getting beyond these forms to a culture's substance may take a considerable amount of digging. Most organizations use one of the two following tools to study and understand their own cultures.

The Audit

During cultural audits, researchers examine situations in which culture asserts itself—role changes, conflicts, and top management behavior. Audits are subjective and qualitative.

"A typical audit," author Schein says, "examines the documents of the official culture: corporate histories, findings from internal and external studies, and standard sources of data on financial performance. The heart of the audit, however, is to uncover values and beliefs through interviews and conversations, and direct observation of people at work. They reveal the systems, stories, and rituals that symbolize the culture."

Areas covered by the audit may include:

- background of top managers, including schooling, time with the organization, job experiences, current duties, career path, and current status
- identification of core values
- how the values are symbolized
- cultural heritage/history since founding
- value differences between the organization and its competitors
- understanding of and extent of buy-in to corporate mission
- the organization's structure and its relation to culture and strategy
- behaviors that reinforce core values
- type of leadership required
- identification of subcultures and their roles

The Survey

Many organizations conduct surveys of their employees that can provide information about the organization's culture. Surveys usually rate degrees of agreement on particular attributes and are quantitative (as opposed to employee attitude surveys, which focus on morale and satisfaction, culture surveys focus on core organizational values).

This type of survey is helpful in identifying trouble spots and the degree to which core values are shared and implemented.

For example, a culture survey conducted by Equitable Life rated the importance of corporate values and how well the value was implemented. Included in the ratings were values such as:

- excellence
- integrity
- career development
- individual development
- mutual trust
- job security
- customer satisfaction
- community involvement
- open and honest communication

Levers for Change

Once management has identified the culture in which it is operating, that culture can be manipulated by using any or all of the "levers" identified by Trice and Beyer. Manipulation of a culture may result in maintaining an existing culture, changing a culture, or instilling a new culture. This can be accomplished by using any of the following means.

■ Ideologies
Ideologies are the substance of a culture and are difficult to both identify and modify. Beliefs and values have "grown" with the organization's history; they can't be easily uprooted. Grafts onto existing cultures need to be modifications of existing beliefs and ones in which top management sincerely believes. Top management must be able to "walk the talk."

■ Forms
Managers should catalog the formal and informal cultural forms that exist within their organizations. The inventory should list things like work settings, language, and logos, as well as the previously discussed myths, legends, sagas, stories, fairy tales, rites, rituals, taboos, and celebrations. Such forms reinforce cultural standards, together with systems of reward, appraisal, and communications. The inventory should also include symbols of who and what are important: dress, office furnishings, who attends meetings, who sits next to whom, and in what order they speak.

■ Socialization
Many organizations use their training and development systems to impart core ideologies. Orientations and rites of passage and enhancement provide clues as to which behaviors are valued by an organization. Role models, leaders, peers, and mentors are also used to socialize members of a culture. "The 80 hours of training IBM provides entry-level managers in their first year," Schein contends, "is spent, in part, 'socializing' newcomers to key corporate values."

■ Subcultures
Managers may be able to use subcultures to reinforce existing cultures or to change cultures. Adding or subtracting occupational subcultures through changing the product or service mix or technology employed will influence both work group culture and the overall culture. Subcultures that share the culture's ideology buttress the organization; managers may want to encourage subcultures by rewarding their leaders. Countercultures can provide alternative values and beliefs when the dominant culture faces a crisis it is unprepared to handle. Managers may find that existing countercultures have developed beliefs and practices that are appropriate to meet the challenge, though they can be resisted even if everyone complains about the dominant culture.

■ Leadership
Cultural leaders need to be effective role models, instill confidence in their followers, to be articulate in expressing values and beliefs, inspire motivation, and have strong convictions about what they are doing. "Cultural leaders," Trice and Beyer say, "need to be more like evangelists than accountants."

■ Environments
Environmental factors include work settings, what products and services to offer, what markets to enter, where and how to obtain needed resources, and where to locate plants. In addition to making decisions about these "objective" environmental factors, managers can influence how the environments are perceived. Managers can frame or interpret environmental factors in such a way that they influence the organization's culture. These efforts at "spin control," or trying to define away outside or environmental messages may remove valid data needed for growth and understanding. It is important to recognize what messages the world is sending about the state of the environment you are

Case Study: The Equitable

In the 1980s, The Equitable, then the third largest U.S. life insurance company, decentralized, reorganized, and undertook a major cultural change to become a "one-stop shop" for financial services. Its strategy included plans to offer a wide range of real estate financial services, decentralize its major insurance operations, and create or eliminate subsidiaries.

These changes shifted financial responsibility downward in the traditional hierarchy and required the cultivation of new beliefs: sensitivity to financial markets, risk taking, acknowledgment and service to customers, commitment to innovation, open communication, and team playing.

To facilitate the change, the human resource department surveyed employees on their current attitudes on work, top management ratings, and the corporation's written and unwritten "rules of the road." The survey revealed values that were not compatible with the planned strategy: Where the new strategy called for risk taking, the survey revealed that a "don't rock the boat" attitude prevailed.

The first step in changing to a "rock the boat" stance occurred when top management identified the following new values that would define The Equitable's ideology:

- be profit- and market-driven
- value customer relationships
- encourage innovation
- recognize and reward performance
- value candid communication
- develop people and encourage teamwork

Based on these values, the human resources department designed an "Employee Development System" (EDS) to address employee needs in the context of the new strategy. The EDS would be closely linked with corporate strategy, while allowing individual units to identify and implement training on specific technical and job-related skills. The system also emphasized a top-down approach to training and reflected the CEO's participative management style.

EDS was a state-of-the-art, companywide training program for all employees and included five core, mandatory training programs and a series of additional, elective programs in finance and technology. The system includes the following:

- Senior management practices that concentrate on analyzing and using strategies based on participative, risk-oriented, entrepreneurial behaviors.

- Advanced management practices, which cover the interpersonal and teamwork skills required to implement a unit strategy tied to the organization's overall goals.

- General management practices covers implementing strategies through tactical plans at the unit level. It explained the new corporate mission, outlined how to identify needed resources, and taught interpersonal skills.

- Management skills for the professional provides an overview of the new strategy while teaching interpersonal and team-building skills.

- Working with others teaches support personnel communications and team skills.

The first two of these were implemented by The Equitable's executive staff. Later decisions required that the other three be left to the individual operating units to implement.

Later surveys found that the two programs offered were both relevant and effective. However, The Equitable found that training, while important, wasn't enough to affect a culture change. In addition to training, new values needed to be reinforced by management behavior, and the systems, procedures, policies, and relationships that sustain the old culture needed to be modified to support the new one.

Adapted from A Manager's Guide to Corporate Culture. *Published by The Conference Board. All rights reserved.*

working in and not try to reframe or spin the information in some preconceived useful way. More than useful or positive data needs to penetrate the culture if it is to build its strength and resiliency. Open systems need to take in all the raw data carefully before filtering this information into ways that fit a particular management agenda.

Creating Change

As Trice and Beyer define it, "culture change is something more deliberate, drastic, and profound than incremental changes or cultural adjustments." William and Gibb Dyer of Cornell University note that cultural change "implies difficult circumstances." Effecting a successful change in culture requires using a combination of many techniques, many of which are also used to maintain or perpetuate existing cultures. A U.S. General Accounting Office study found that the following techniques, the first two of which are critical to success, are used:

■ Gaining Top Management Support
Senior officials must articulate and live by organizational values and beliefs to demonstrate to employees that top management is committed to making permanent culture changes and is not merely paying lip service to those changes.

■ Training
Organizations that place a high value on training as a tool successfully reinforce their missions, values, and guiding principles. Management development, including appraisal and appraisal training, a more open style of management, and leadership training are integral to the cultural change process.

■ Value and Belief Statements
Articulating an organization's values and distributing a written statement of those values to employees is an important technique. Merck, for example, used its core ideology to guide its business decisions, including how to handle the Mectizan crisis described earlier. CEO Roy Vagelos described the purpose of Merck by looking one hundred years into the future:

...no matter what changes might have occurred in the Company, I know we would find one thing had remained the same—and the thing that matters most: the. . .spirit of Merck people. . . I believe this, above all, because Merck's dedication to fighting disease, relieving suffering, and helping people is a righteous cause—one that inspires people to dream of doing great things...It is a timeless cause.

■ Communicating Desired Values and Beliefs
Although all of these techniques relate to communication, organizations often use weekly or monthly meetings, posters, newsletters, pamphlets, magazines, in-house television networks, and videotapes to communicate their values and beliefs. Annual or biannual questionnaires measure employee perceptions of the company's success in living up to its stated beliefs and values.

■ Management Style
Companies that want to change their cultures often have to change their management style and perhaps even their organizational structure. For example, to change its reputation for poor customer service, Chrysler came up with a program of cultural change—Customer One. This program involved ideas from suppliers, customers, designers, assembly line workers, and mechanics all working together to set goals and improve quality. This was done with the same people, but by instigating a different organizational culture.

■ Organizational Structure
Companies also find that organizational structure reflects its culture. Although reorganizing is not a mechanism for cultural change, it is part and parcel of a change strategy. The most common forms of structural change include decentralizing, shutting down old divisions or plants, and downsizing headquarters.

■ Rewards, Incentives, and Promotions
Some organizations offer rewards, incentives, and promotions to employees whose behavior supports the desired organizational culture. The rewards are seen as ways to encourage similar behavior in other employees and help to perpetuate or change values.

■ Organizational Gatherings
Some organizations use "gatherings" to explain their values and beliefs to workers. At Disney, for instance, all employees must attend a "Disney Traditions" orientation seminar. During these sessions, trainers ask questions about Disney's characters, history, mythology to their employees, or "cast members." They have their own language, which describes job as a "part," uniform as a "costume," the work shift as a "performance," and so

Techniques for Changing Culture

"An organization's decision to change its culture is generally triggered by a specific event or situation," according to a U.S. Government Accounting Office study. These events or situations range from international competition to severe budget restrictions.

The study group comprised nine large companies and five academics who have studied corporate culture. The companies studied were Federal Express, Johnson & Johnson, 3M, AT&T, Corning, DuPont, Ford, IBM, and Motorola. The academics were Terrence E. Deal, Peabody College of Vanderbilt University; J. Steven Ott, University of Maine; Vijay Sathe, Claremont College; Edgar H. Schein, Sloan School of Management, Massachusetts Institute of Technology; and Alan L. Wilkins, Brigham Young University.

The survey found that changing an organization's culture is a long-term effort—it generally takes between five and 10 years to complete. The survey respondents also isolated two key components of a successful change in culture:

- Top management must be totally committed to the change in both words and deeds.

- Organizations must provide training that promotes and develops skills related to their desired values and beliefs.

The following table shows the techniques used by the respondents and their degree of importance:

Degree of Importance	Technique
Very Great	Display top management commitment and support for values and beliefs. Train employees to convey and develop skills related to values and beliefs.
Great	Develop a statement of values and beliefs. Communicate values and beliefs to employees. Use a management style compatible with values and beliefs. Offer rewards, incentives, and promotions to encourage behavior compatible with values and beliefs. Convey and support values and beliefs at organizational gatherings. Make the organization's structure compatible with values and beliefs.[a] Set up systems, procedures, and processes compatible with values and beliefs.[a]
Moderate	Replace or change responsibilities of employees who do not support desired values or beliefs.[a] Use stories, legends, or myths to convey values and beliefs. Make heroes or heroines of exemplars of values and beliefs.
Some	Recruit employees who possess or will readily accept values and beliefs.[a] Use slogans to symbolize values and beliefs. Assign a manager or group primary responsibility for efforts to change or perpetuate a culture.[a]

[a]Company officials' views of the importance of this technique varied widely.

Note: DuPont based its responses on techniques used in its Materials, Logistics, and Services Division, which was at the forefront of its culture change. Motorola based its responses on its six sigma efforts to reduce defects in products and services to no more that 3.4 per million.

From Organizational Culture: Techniques Companies Use to Perpetuate or Change Beliefs and Values, *GAO/NSIAD-92-105, February 1992, U.S. Government Accounting Office, Washington, DC 20548.*

forth. All of this reinforces the Disney ideology and keeping the "magic" in the Magic Kingdom.

■ Systems, Procedures, and Processes

The systems, procedures, and processes used by an organization must be compatible with its values and beliefs. The pay system is one way to reinforce concretely the new ideology. Many organizations, for example, have tied pay to productivity. In another instance, Federal Express has developed mechanisms—such as a no-layoff policy, promotions from within, and a grievance-airing meeting—to support its stated commitment to employee satisfaction.

■ Staff Changes

When employees do not support the existing or changing culture, some organizations replace them or change their responsibilities. These "outlaws" are often lured by early retirement programs and generous outplacement plans. It is important to maintain the individual's self-respect and dignity when making this change.

■ Stories, Myths, and Legends

Organizations in the process of changing the culture should also change the existing legends to reinforce the new values. The stories can be told in meetings, employee newsletters, or a book of successes.

■ Heroes and Heroines

Some firms make heroes or heroines out of employees who exemplify their values and beliefs. The making of heroes or heroines usually occurs through storytelling and rites—the presentation of a public reward for good behavior.

■ Hiring the Right People

Recruiting individuals who believe in or are willing to accept the organization's ideology makes indoctrination into the culture easier. Currently few, if any, organizations have processes in place to ensure success in this effort. It is important, however, to communicate the organization's current and desired values and both positive and negative aspects of the job to prospective employees. This may help in attracting and retaining workers who share the organization's beliefs.

■ Slogans

Slogans symbolize an organization's core beliefs. 3M, for example, cites its slogans: "People count at 3M"; "Innovation working for you"; "Take small steps"; and "Make a little, sell a little"; as helping make employees proud of where they work.

■ Assigning a Culture Manager

A person or group may be assigned to help instill the new values inherent in cultural change issues. Most top managers, however, avoid taking this step because they believe many employees should be involved in their culture change or perpetuation efforts.

Next Steps

An organization may shift and change, but a truly visionary company reinforces its core values and beliefs and commits itself to following this ideology. Merck, for instance, is so successful because it has aligned its words with its actions since its founding in 1891. Collins and Porras in *Built to Last*, quoted Merck's director of science and technology policy, Jeffrey L. Sturchio, as follows:

"I used to work at another major American corporation before coming to Merck. The basic difference I see between the two companies is rhetoric versus reality. The other company touted values and visions and all the rest, but there was a big difference between rhetoric and reality. At Merck, there is no difference."

What is your company's organizational culture? What attitudes and beliefs have influenced your workplace? Are differences honored and old values respected and upheld? Is your organization "built to last" with a solid foundation or is it unfinished, unbalanced, or unstable? What might be missing? What really counts in your company's culture?

The Past Is Prologue

Managers who plan radical changes in their organizational culture may find that "you can't get there from here." To be successful, new cultures must evolve from existing cultures; new cultures can't be superimposed on existing cultures that espouse different ideologies. An organization considering significant change would "do well to...both honor the past and learn how to grow in new ways," assert Alan Wilkins and Nigel Bristow of Brigham Young University. They suggest the following guidelines for change that honors the past:

Return to the past for inspiration and instruction. Recalling the values that made the organization successful initially will remind employees of what it's like to be successful while emphasizing founding values.

Get back to basics. Top management may "confess" that they've strayed from the founding values; others may simply actively remind staff of the values and reinforce them.

Find examples of success within the current culture. Subcultures and countercultures may exist that can serve as models for change. These groups may have faced the challenge and overcome it.

Label eras. Managers who seek to change the culture will give employees a touchstone if they name the existing culture and the upcoming era. This gives employees a sense of continuity.

Mourn the loss of the past. Until people can mourn and "bury" the past, they're unable to move forward. Many organizations sponsor ceremonies to mark the end of one era and the beginning of a new one.

Scoring for Organizational Indicators Test

Count the number of times you answered "yes" to the questions on page 27.

16-20 Congratulations! You work in a high-performance culture. Your "human organization should provide a strong base for implementing organizational strategy," Schuster notes.

11-15 You could probably improve your culture by increasing attention to managing culture. Such increased attention should enable your "human organization to achieve higher performance and should pay off on the bottom line," says Schuster.

10 or less Your organization is "falling seriously short of using culture for maximum competitive advantage," Schuster observes, adding that *"at best*, culture may be a nonfactor in the accomplishment of organizational strategy; more likely it is a hindrance or a block."

References & Resources

Articles

Allerton, Haidee. "Professional Development the Disney Way." *Training & Development,* May 1997, pp. 50-56.

Albert, Michael. "Transmitting Corporate Culture Through Case Studies." *Personnel,* August 1987, pp. 71-73.

Alexander, George P. "Establishing Shared Values Through Management Training Programs." *Training & Development Journal,* February 1987, pp. 45-47.

Brown, Abby. "Is Ethics Good Business?" *Personnel Administrator (UK),* February 1987, pp. 71-74.

Burack, Elmer H. "Changing the Company Culture—The Role of Human Resource Development." *Long Range Planning,* February 1991, pp. 88-95.

Cacioppe, Ron. "Bringing the Tribe into the Bureaucracy." *Training & Development Journal,* December 1989, pp. 70-74.

Campbell, Andrew. "The Power of Mission: Aligning Strategy and Culture." *Planning Review,* September/October 1992, pp. 10-12, 63.

Christensen, Gail. "Managing Workforce Diversity: Changing Culture at South Seas Plantation." *Cornell Hotel & Restaurant Administration Quarterly,* August 1988, pp. 30-34.

Cohen, Sacha. "On Becoming Virtual." *Training & Development,* May 1997, pp. 30-37.

Collins, James C., and Jerry I. Porras. "Building Your Company's Vision." *Harvard Business Review,* September/October 1996, pp. 65-77.

Cooney, Barry D. "Japan and America: Culture Counts." *Training & Development Journal,* August 1989, pp. 58-61.

Cox, Allan. "Linking Purpose and People." *Training & Development,* March 1996, pp. 67-68.

Crabb, Stephen. "The Way to Cable Change." *Personnel Management (UK),* June 1990, pp. 50-53.

Cullen, John B., et al. "An Ethical Weather Report: Assessing the Organization's Ethical Climate." *Organizational Dynamics,* Autumn 1989, pp. 50-61.

DeLisi, Peter S. "Lessons from the Steel Axe: Culture, Technology, and Organizational Change." *Sloan Management Review,* Fall 1990, pp. 83-93.

Deluga, Ronald J. "Relationship of Transformational and Transactional Leadership With Employee Influencing Strategies." *Group and Organization Studies,* December 1988, pp. 456-467.

Denison, Daniel R. "What Is the Difference Between Organizational Culture and Organizational Climate? A Native's Point of View on a Decade of Paradigm Wars." *Academy of Management Review,* July 1996, pp. 619-654.

Doktor, Robert H. "Asian and American CEOs: A Comparative Study." *Organizational Dynamics,* Winter 1990, pp. 46-56.

Drake, Bruce H., and Eileen Drake. "Ethical and Legal Aspects of Managing Corporate Cultures." *California Management Review.* Winter 1988, pp. 107-123.

Dreyfuss, Joel. "Reinventing IBM." *Fortune,* August 14, 1989, pp. 30-39.

Dumaine, Brian. "Creating a New Company Culture." *Fortune,* January 15, 1990, pp. 127-131.

———. "Those High-Flying Pepsico Managers." *Fortune,* April 10, 1989, pp. 78-80, 84-86.

Duncan, W. Jack. "Organizational Culture: 'Getting a Fix' on an Elusive Concept.," *Academy of Management Executive,* 1989, pp. 229-236.

Durrance, Bonnie. "Stories at Work." *Training & Development,* February 1997, pp. 25-29.

Ettorre, Barbara. "On the future of Work and an End to the 'Century of the Organization.'" *Organizational Dynamics,* Summer 1996, pp. 15-26.

Feldman, Steven P. "How Organizational Culture Can Affect Innovation." *Organizational Dynamics,* Summer 1988, pp. 57-68.

Filipczak, Bob. "Beyond the Gates at Microsoft." *Training,* September 1992, pp. 37-44.

Fisher, Kevin, and Joe A. Spillane. "Quality and Competitiveness." *Training & Development,* September 1991, pp. 19-24.

Fitzgerald, Thomas. "Can Change in Organizational Culture Really be Managed?" *Organizational Dynamics,* Autumn 1988, pp. 5-15.

Flynn, Gillian. "It Takes Values to Capitalize on Change." *Workforce,* April 1997, pp. 27-34.

Fullerton, Hance, and Colin Price. "Culture Change in the NHS." *Personnel Management (UK),* March 1991, pp. 50-53.

Galagan, Patricia. "Bringing Spirit Back to the Workplace: An Interview with W. Mathew Juechter." *Training & Development Journal,* September 1988, pp. 35-39.

———. "Growth: Mapping Its Patterns and Periods." *Training & Development Journal,* November 1989, pp. 40-48.

References & Resources

———. "How to Take on Top Management and Win." *Training & Development,*. June 1992, pp. 25-28.

Gellerman, Saul W. "Managing Ethics from the Top Down." *Sloan Management Review,* Winter 1989, pp. 73-79.

Gibb, Allan A. "Enterprise Culture—Its Meaning and Implications for Education and Training." *Journal of European Industrial Training (UK),* 1987, pp. 3-38.

Goffee, Rob, and Gareth Jones. "What Holds the Modern Company Together?" *Harvard Business Review,* November/December 1996, pp. 133-148.

Goldstein, Jeffrey, and Marjorie Leopold. "Corporate Culture vs. Ethnic Culture." *Personnel Journal,* November 1990, pp. 83-92.

Griesinger, Donald W. "The Human Side of Economic Organization," *Academy of Management Review.* July 1990, pp. 478-499.

Harrison, Edward L., and Paul H. Pietri. "Achieving Cultural Change Through Management Training and Survey Feedback." *Organization Development Journal,* Winter 1991, pp. 66-73.

Konrad, Walecia. "Welcome to the Woman-Friendly Company." *Business Week,* August 6, 1990, pp. 48-55.

Kovach, Barbara E., and James Parish. "How to Lead the Metamorphosis." *Training & Development Journal,* December 1988, pp. 40-43.

Lei, David, et al. "Global Strategy and Reward Systems: The Key Roles of Management Development and Corporate Culture." *Organizational Dynamics,* Autumn 1990, pp. 27-41.

O'Neal, Paul E. "Transforming Managers for Organizational Change." *Training & Development Journal,* July 1990, pp. 87-90.

Owens, Reginald. "Diversity: A Bottom-line Issue." *Workforce,* March 1997, pp. 3-5.

Payne, Roy. "Taking Stock of Corporate Culture." *Personnel Management,* July 1991, pp. 26-29.

Pearce, Craig L. and Charles P. Osmond. "Metaphors for Change: the ALPs Model of Change Management." *Organizational Dynamics,* Winter 1996, pp. 23-34.

Plant, Roger, and Mark Ryan. "Managing Your Corporate Culture." *Training & Development Journal,* September 1988, pp. 35-39.

Rubin, Irwin and Robert Inguagiato. "Changing the Work Culture." *Training & Development,* July 1991, pp. 57-60.

Schein, Edgar H. "What You Need to Know About Organizational Culture." *Training & Development Journal,* January 1986, pp. 30-33.

Schriber, Jacquelyn B. and Barbara A. Gutek. "Some Time Dimensions of Work: Measurement of an Underlying Aspect of Organization Culture." *Journal of Applied Psychology,* November 1987, pp. 642-650.

Schuster, Frederick E. "Does Your Organization Have a High Performance Culture?" *HR Horizons,* Winter 1991, pp. 20-23.

Shapiro, George L. and Maryan S. Schall. "Rhetorical Rules and Organization—Cultures: Identification, Maintenance, and Change." *Human Resource Development Quarterly,* Winter 1990, pp. 321-337.

Simmons, John. "Participatory Management: Lessons from the Leaders." *Management Review,* December 1990, pp. 54-58.

Sinetar, Marsha. "Building Trust Into Corporate Relationships." *Organizational Dynamics,* Winter 1988, pp. 73-79.

Solomon, Charlene M. "24-hour Employees." *Personnel Journal,* August 1991, pp. 56-63.

Sonnenberg, Frank K. and Beverly Goldberg. "It's a Great Idea, But..." *Training & Development,* March 1992, pp. 65-68.

Spruell, Geraldine. "Will Competition Knock the People Out of People Express?" *Training & Development Journal,* May 1986, pp. 50-54.

Stamps, David. "Relaxed Fit." *Training,* October 1996, pp. 90-100.

Sutton, Robert I. and Meryl Reis Louis. "How Selecting and Socializing Newcomers Influence Insiders." *Human Resource Management,* Fall 1987, pp. 347-361.

Tichy, Noel M. "Training as a Lever for Change." *New Management.* Winter 1987, pp. 39-41.

———. "Simultaneous Transformation and CEO Succession: Key to Global Competitiveness." *Organizational Dynamics,* Summer 1996, pp. 45-59.

Trickett, David. "How to Use a Values Audit." *Training & Development,* March 1997, pp. 34-38.

Upton, Richard. "Xerox Copies the Message on Quality." *Personnel Management (UK),* April 1987, pp. 34-37.

References & Resources

Articles, continued

Veltrop, Bill and Karin Harrington. "Roadmap to New Organizational Territory." *Training & Development Journal,* June 1988, pp. 23-33.

Verespej, Michael A. "Zero Tolerance." *Industry Week,* January 6, 1997, pp. 24-28.

Vicere, Albert A. "The Changing Paradigm for Executive Development." *Journal of Management Development (UK),* 1991, pp. 44-47.

Vogt, Judith F. and Stephen J. Griffith. "Team Development and Proactive Change: Theory and Training Implications." *Organization Development Journal,* Winter 1988, pp. 81-87.

Wilkins, Alan L. and Nigel J. Bristow. "For Successful Organizational Culture, Honor Your Past." *Academy of Management Executive,* August 1987, pp. 221-227.

Wilkins, Alan L. and W. Gibb Dyer, Jr. "Toward Culturally Sensitive Theories of Culture Change." *Academy of Management Review,* October 1988, pp. 522-533.

Wilson, James A. and Nancy S. Elman. "Organizational Benefits of Mentoring." *Academy of Management Executive,* November 1990, pp. 88-94.

Wisdom, Barry L. and D. Keith Denton. "Manager as Teacher." *Training & Development,* December 1991, pp. 54-58.

Woodlands Group. "Respecting Beliefs and Values." *Training & Development Journal,* January 1989, pp. 74-76.

Zatz, David A. "Harnessing the Power of Cultural Change." *ANSOM,* February 1994.

Zemke, Ron. "The Call of Community." *Training,* March 1996, pp. 24-30.

Books

Adizes, Ichak. *Corporate Lifecycles: How and Why Corporations Grow and Die and What to Do About It.* Englewood Cliffs, New Jersey: Prentice-Hall, 1988.

Allcorn, Seth. *Workplace Superstars in Resistant Organizations.* New York: Quorum Books, 1991.

Allen, Robert F. and Robert L. Craig (eds.). *Training and Development Handbook,* 3d ed. New York: McGraw-Hill, 1987.

Bolman, Lee G. and Terrence E. Deal. *Reframing Organizations: Artistry, Choice, and Leadership.* San Francisco: Jossey-Bass, 1991.

Buono, Anthony F. and James L. Bowditch. *The Human Side of Mergers and Acquisitions.* San Francisco: Jossey-Bass, 1989.

Crosby, Philip B. *The Eternally Successful Organization.* New York: McGraw-Hill, 1988.

Davis, Stanley M. *Managing Corporate Culture.* Cambridge, Massachusetts: Ballinger Publishing, 1984.

Denison, Daniel R. *Corporate Culture and Organizational Effectiveness.* New York: John Wiley & Sons, 1990.

DuBrin, Andrew J. *Foundations of Organizational Behavior: An Applied Perspective.* Englewood Cliffs, New Jersey: Prentice-Hall, 1984.

Falsey, Thomas A. *Corporate Philosophies and Mission Statements.* New York: Quorum Books, 1989.

Frank, Allan D. and Judi L. Brownell. *Organizational Communication and Behavior: Communicating to Improve Performance.* New York: Holt, Rhinehart, and Winston, 1989.

Glidewell, John C. *Corporate Cultures: Research Implications for Human Resource Development.* Alexandria, Virginia: American Society for Training & Development, 1986.

Harvey, Jerry B. *The Abilene Paradox.* Lexington, Massachusetts: Lexington Books, 1988.

Hiam, Alexander. *Closing the Quality Gap: Lessons from America's Leading Companies.* Englewood Cliffs, New Jersey: Prentice-Hall, 1992.

Jablin, Fredric M. (ed.). *Handbook of Organizational Communication.* Newbury Park, California: Sage Publications, 1987.

Kets de Vries, et al. *Organizations on the Couch: Clinical Perspectives on Organizational Behavior and Change.* San Francisco: Jossey-Bass, 1991.

Marquardt, Michael J. (ed.). *Internal HRD Annual,* Volume 3. Alexandria, Virginia: American Society for Training & Development, 1987.

References & Resources

Mink, Oscar G., et al. *Developing and Managing Open Organizations.* Austin, Texas: Learning Concepts, 1979.

Mintzberg, Henry. *Mintzberg on Management.* New York: Free Press, 1989.

Neuhauser, Peg. *Tribal Warfare in Organizations.* Cambridge, Massachusetts: Ballinger Publishing, 1988.

Organizational Culture: Techniques Companies Use to Perpetuate or Change Beliefs and Values. Washington, DC: U.S. General Accounting Office, 1992.

Raelin, Joseph A. *Clash of Culture: Managers and Professionals.* Boston, Massachusetts: Harvard Business School Press, 1986.

Reidenbach, R. Eric. *Business Ethics: Where Profits Meet Value Systems.* Englewood Cliffs, New Jersey: Prentice-Hall, 1989.

Roth Jr., William F. *A Systems Approach to Quality Improvement.* New York: Praeger, 1992.

Schien, Lawrence. *A Manager's Guide to Corporate Culture.* New York: The Conference Board, 1989.

Shapiro, Eileen C. *How Corporate Truths Become Competitive Traps.* New York: John Wiley & Sons, 1991.

Ulrich, David, and Dale Lake. *Organizational Capability: Competing from the Inside Out.* New York: John Wiley & Sons, 1990.

Wilkins, Alan L. *Developing Corporate Character.* San Francisco: Jossey-Bass, 1989.

Info-lines

Finn, Tom "Valuing and Managing Diversity." No. 9305 (revised 1999).

Marquardt, Michael. "Action Learning." No. 9704.

———. "16 steps to Becoming a Learning Organization." (revised 1997). No. 9602

Shaffer, Rima. "Principles of Organization Development." No. 8812 (revised 1999).

Smith, Warren. "Managing Change." No. 8910 (out of print).

Younger, Sandra Millers. "How to Develop a Vision." No. 9107 (revised 1999).

Zulauf, Carol. "Systems Thinking." No. 9703.

Internet Sites

American Society for Training & Development
http://www.astd.org/

http://webtrax.com.au/

http://www.sagepub.co.uk/books/details/b003061.html/

http://www.udel.edu/johnc/courses/iporg/com455.html/

http://www.baclass.panam.edu/courses/mana3335/culture.html/

http://www.gwu.edu/~ceep/g-docments/2080.html/

http://www.surcon.com/Enhanced/TheSurconReport/Report0697.html/

http://www.ioc.army.mil/io/qa/Qae/Culture/Culthtml.htm/

http://me.mit.edu/groups/lfm/working_papers/1996_abstracts/smit_abstract_1996.html/

http://delphi.colorado.edu/~itdtq/managing-diversity.html/

http://delphi.colorado.edu/~irm/stds/ciw_user/organization/culture.html/

http://www.anderson.ucla.edu/research/conferences/scos/abstract/tammerev.htm/

http://z.simplenet.com/od/a/culture2.html

Job Aid

Management Style Diagnostic

Determining your organization's or unit's management style will go a long way to defining the culture in which you work. The following multiple choice questions will help you determine your primary and secondary work cultures.

1. What or who determines the criteria for success?

a) The boss

b) The rule book

c) The group

d) The occupation

e) The customer

2. What is the organization's central theme?

a) Flexibility, adaptability

b) Order, predictability

c) Involvement, commitment, participation

d) Knowledge, expertise

e) Quality, service, dependability

3. How does information flow in the organization?

a) Random, arbitrary

b) Formal, vertical

c) Free flow

d) Through the occupation

e) Trial and error

4. What are the bases of power?

a) Charisma

b) Political struggles

c) Interpersonal competence

d) Expertise

e) Commercial success

5. How are conflicts resolved?

a) The boss

b) Rules and procedures

c) Consensus

d) Professional autonomy

e) Centralized for values; decentralized for action

Scoring

Count up the number of times you answered a, b, c, d, or e. The letter with the highest count is the dominant culture; the second highest score is the secondary culture.

a = Founder-father
b = Bureaucratic
c = Participative
d = Professional
e = Managerial-entrepreneurial

Change Management

Issue 9904

A U T H O R :

Stella Louise Cowan, M.Ed.
Tel.: 313.393.0050
Fax: 313.393.0051
E-mail: lndybridge@msn.com

Stella Cowan has worked in training design and delivery and organizational development for over 14 years. Her work experience is vast—ranging from acting as a learning systems consultant to a leadership education specialist. She now operates a business in instructional design. Stella is also an adjunct professor in management at Spring Arbor College and Baker College.

Editor
Cat Sharpe

Associate Editor
Sabrina E. Hicks

Production Design
Anne Morgan

ASTD Internal Consultant
Phil Anderson

Change Management

Change: The Inevitable Reality

Organizations are under siege by a relentless business environment—relentless due to its ability to change at an exponential rate. As a result, negative realities such as the following persist:

- shrinking market share
- increasing customer demands
- continuing inefficient, obsolete processes
- altering workforce due to demographic changes

Creating solutions to harness these changes and providing practitioners to guide the helm of change are hot topics for people like us in the training or human resources (HR) profession. Organizations need change practitioners who can not only conceive of the broad, *aerial* strategy but can also break down this strategy into specific action-oriented activities that move the change forward (that is, operationalize the strategy). We call this the *ground* view.

You must have an aerial, big picture view of your organization's approach to change. This big picture falls flat, however, if you do not operationalize it. Listed below are the key players in managing the change for your organization:

- organizational development specialist
- trainer
- HR expert

Although there is no magic elixir to ease organizational change, certain tactics can help you manage your organization's change efforts. Use this issue of *Info-line* as a primer on change management tactics and the skills needed to facilitate change and implementation roadblocks. This issue includes a number of tools, hands-on examples, and models for change practitioners to use as resources and ideas. With the continued increase in mergers, downsizing, and reengineering, these tools are beneficial because a high-level of such change practitioner skills are extremely valuable and marketable.

The Broad or Aerial View

The emphasis of this *Info-line* is the tactical side of change management; however, we must start by taking a look at a typical broad view. The *Six-Phase Change Strategy Model* sidebar on the following page represents the phases of change along a continuum. It shows that progress can be forward or backward, depending on what is going on in the organization.

You must remember that change is incremental relative to both the redesign or reengineering of processes and the transformation of employee attitudes and behaviors. Attitudes and behaviors such as sliding trust, increasing disengagement, and growing fear are challenging to manage and require most of the actions described in the six steps of the model. The change manager (whether he or she is an organizational development specialist, trainer, or HR practitioner) supports forward movement through programs and active advocacy of change. The bottom line is that successful change demands a multi-pronged approach.

The Dynamics of Change

Having a broad, aerial view for the change process is just the first step. You need perspective on the challenge of moving each employee through the different phases of change acceptance, which we will refer to as the Adaptation/Acceptance Spectrum (consult the sidebar on page 49). Keep in mind this phrase: "Change is a process, not an event." Change takes time and typically occurs in overlapping increments—plus, it does not occur as a result of a single effort.

Change is an emotional experience for those involved, and people adjust to change at different rates. It can bring pain, confusion, uncertainty, guilt (for change survivors), and even excitement for those who see personal advantages in it. Understanding the characteristics of each phase of the Adaptation/Acceptance Spectrum helps you manage the change in your organization.

Six-Phase Change Strategy Model

This model depicts each phase as an independent item. It is important to remember, however, that the actions involved are not necessarily independent of each other. Some can occur concurrently. For example, monitoring impact (phase 4) and responding to feedback (phase 5) should occur at almost all points. In addition, actions like training and communications are common threads, punctuating most of the phases.

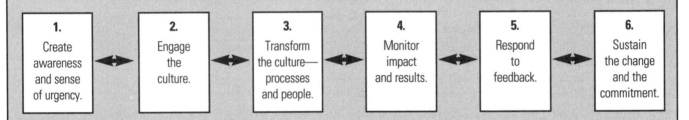

1. Create awareness and sense of urgency. ◀▶ **2.** Engage the culture. ◀▶ **3.** Transform the culture—processes and people. ◀▶ **4.** Monitor impact and results. ◀▶ **5.** Respond to feedback. ◀▶ **6.** Sustain the change and the commitment.

The Six Phases

Phase 1: Create awareness and a sense of urgency. Communicate information on the need for change on a consistent and timely basis. Communicate a clear vision for the organization's future. Share the business case for the specific change strategies selected. Share the financial picture and financial recovery plan to the extent possible.

Phase 2: Engage the culture. Implement programs like town meetings, merger or integration hot lines with prerecorded updates, support circles, and cross-division and level change leadership councils. Create avenues for employee input and involvement.

Phase 3: Transform the culture—processes and people. Implement specific actions such as training, coaching, job counseling, redesign of performance system, and restructure of job roles.

Phase 4: Monitor impact and results. Obtain and analyze data on employees' adaptation to the change, affect of the change on meeting customer requirements, and degree of progress on system or process modifications.

Phase 5: Respond to feedback. Make on-going, appropriate adjustments to the change strategies and tactics.

Phase 6: Sustain the change and the commitment. Ensure that you align HR systems like recruitment, rewards, training, and involvement to carry the new culture forward. Ensure management systems (like decision making and communication) reflect the new culture. Ensure the physical structure of the organization is consistent with the needs of the new culture.

Phase 1: Thrusting into the Unknown

For the most part, people like the comfort and perceived certainty of their current state. Managing their move from rejection to acceptance (and ideally to embrace) takes time and depends on the stimuli prompting the change. As shown in the sidebar on the following page, change begins for employees with the act of "thrusting" them into the unknown or uncertain. The unknown or uncertain can be any number of events:

- a new procedure
- a change in job responsibilities
- a change in reporting relationships
- a change in business practices
- the loss of a job

People tend to freeze or become paralyzed in this phase of the spectrum.

The literature and theories on involvement indicate that people are more likely to resist change in which they have no input, which is disturbing because people are usually put in a new situation unexpectedly and without their input or involvement. Input or involvement engenders a sense of ownership of the situation. Such ownership does

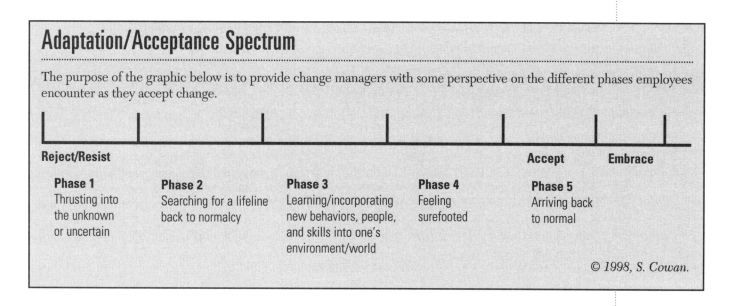

Adaptation/Acceptance Spectrum

The purpose of the graphic below is to provide change managers with some perspective on the different phases employees encounter as they accept change.

Reject/Resist   **Accept**   **Embrace**

Phase 1
Thrusting into
the unknown
or uncertain

Phase 2
Searching for a lifeline
back to normalcy

Phase 3
Learning/incorporating
new behaviors, people,
and skills into one's
environment/world

Phase 4
Feeling
surefooted

Phase 5
Arriving back
to normal

© 1998, S. Cowan.

not mean that employees who are required to change expect to be the decision makers. But it does mean this: They want you to consider their ideas, and they want you to inform them about events leading to decisions affecting them.

Even if the situation of change cannot be avoided, letting them know ahead of time can lessen the resistance. When it comes to communication and involvement, more is better. To manage the fear of the unknown and lessen resistance, tactics such as the following will help as you communicate change:

- regularly scheduled voice or e-mail messages on the state of the change

- cross-functional reengineering teams with rotating membership

- periodic focus groups to solicit ideas

- change readiness or climate surveys

Phase 2: Searching for Normalcy

Despite communication and involvement, the "Searching for a Lifeline Back to Normalcy" phase can be difficult and long lasting. Employees may understand the change and feel involved to some degree, but grabbing that lifeline is no easy task.

Even at this stage, people are still somewhat frozen or paralyzed by change. Your role in change management is pivotal in constructing the lifeline.

The lifeline consists of support actions needed to facilitate release from the frozen state. This does not imply that there is a quick fix. But, support actions like the ones described below can help the thaw.

Coping skills. Effective coping techniques are important for managing change. Coping techniques include the following:

- implementing stress and grief management (typically, people experience loss and go through the stages of grief when responding to a drastic change like job elimination)

- handling ambiguity

- confronting fears

Facilitator-led workshops, counseling, videotapes, and audiotapes are formats for teaching coping skills. Employee assistance providers can also support this effort. Keep in mind that coping skills are valuable through the entire change cycle. Change is a process, and as it unfolds it brings new disruptions to handle.

Decision making. If jobs are relocating or changing substantially and employees have the opportunity to decide whether they want to relocate or retrain, the quality of their decision making is important. That is why items like a worksheet or pamphlet containing the pertinent decision factors and tips for reaching the best personal decision are valuable. They help employees feel as if they have some control over their circumstances.

Emotional support. You cannot underestimate the value of emotional support. People need understanding and empathy (not to be confused with sympathy). They need to know that although you cannot necessarily fix their pain, you can relate to it. Moreover, people need to connect with others experiencing similar circumstances.

Support groups, either in person or virtual, can address this need. The groups can be informal or facilitated. The group format provides an arena for expressing and receiving empathy and for divesting emotionally. Employees that benefit particularly from the group format are the survivors of downsizing. Very often, these people suffer from *survivor's guilt* and need their own special emotional support.

Career or job planning. Today, more than ever, people need to be adept at career or job planning. One of the most difficult changes for people can be workforce transition (that is, movement of people to different jobs, elimination of jobs, or transfer of jobs). People are sometimes wedded to their job with no concept of how to transfer their skill sets to a different job. Understanding the concept of transferring skill sets opens up new opportunities for the individual and the organization. In fact, from the organization's viewpoint, redeployment of resources can be a strategic option.

Getting to "Normal"

The road from "Phase 3: Learning/Incorporating New Behaviors" to "Phase 5: Arriving Back to Normal" requires a host of actions. However, it bears repeating that there is no magic formula. The information described under "Change Management Skills" and "Operationalizing the Change Strategy" speak to those actions.

Change Management Skills

Successful change management weaves together two key threads:

1. People considerations (for example, emotions associated with job or work elimination or survival).

2. Process considerations (such as restructuring of tasks and responsibilities).

Change is a two-sided coin that involves both people transformation and business strategy innovation. Sometimes, however, the emphasis on reengineering the processes and systems eclipses the people side. This is a mistake. The human or high-touch side of change management is a necessary ingredient. An effective change manager, therefore, is a combination of strategist, process consultant, diagnostician, and *humanist*. Characteristics of a successful change manager include the following:

- appreciates that organizational change unearths interpersonal or emotional issues (that is, the "people" side of change)

- understands the implications of change to production and management systems

- knows how to take in, sort through, and frame information in a way that creates a foundation for a change strategy

- can build an appropriate strategy that integrates the "people" and the "process" side of change management

- can operationalize the broad strategy into specific tactics

More specifically, the 12 groups of behaviors described in the *Implementation Skills* sidebar at right are key to success at change management. The behaviors are particularly relevant to the critical objective of balancing people transformation with business innovation or process redesign.

Implementation Skills

Having a sound, detailed plan; top leadership support; the resources; and the manpower for your organization's change is ammunition for success. But to win the battle, you need certain skills to implement the change effectively. While there is no definitive list of skills for change managers, the list below is applicable to fueling an atmosphere of change and implementing appropriate change tactics. Also, depending on your organization's particular change situation (for example, wide scale versus limited or targeted change, merger versus spin-off of a division or business segment), the frequency and extent you use the skills may vary.

Skill Sets	Behaviors
1. Thinking Analytically	● Evaluating data or information systematically to identify surface, as well as underlying, causes of problems (for example, performance gaps or process misalignment). ● Assessing the impact of solutions and making appropriate modifications.
2. Seeing the "Big Picture"	● Looking beyond details to see the overarching goals and results. ● Understanding the impact of business decisions on the entire change strategy. ● Making appropriate modifications to the general strategy based on business decisions and customer input.
3. Thinking Out-of-the-Box	● Designing new or innovative ways to address organization initiatives and customer needs.
4. Using Technology	● Using existing or new technology to design products, create solutions, deliver programs, and market services.
5. Using Human Relations	● Working collaboratively with others to build understanding and trust and to achieve common goals. ● Establishing and maintaining rapport with individuals and groups.
6. Learning Continuously	● Being self-directed and persistent in pursuing new information, technology, and ideas.
7. Creating Partnerships/Networks	● Building ownership and support for change among affected individuals or groups.
8. Thinking Holistically	● Recognizing that an organization is a living, breathing entity. ● Identifying the parts of an organizational process or operation. ● Understanding how the parts fit together and the impact of misalignment of one part on another. ● Understanding the impact of modifying one part on another.
9. Using Project Leadership Methods	● Acting as a lead contact or focal point for components (for example, program, intervention, or event) of the change strategy. ● Directing the activities of others contributing to the component. ● Overseeing project deadlines, deliverables, and customer expectations. ● Adapting to constraints and unexpected roadblocks.
10. Leveraging Power/Influence	● Establishing and using a power base through unique knowledge or expertise or through alignment with power brokers in the organization.
11. Creating Solutions	● Customizing or designing solutions that best fit the problem. ● Implementing the solutions. ● Tracking the impact of the solutions and making adjustments as appropriate.
12. Responding to Clients	● Interpreting client needs and expectations through various actions (for example, feedback system, survey, and consistent in-person contact). ● Developing effective solutions (for example, coaching, training, or intervention) to close the gap if needs or expectations are not met.

As is evident by the 12 groups of behaviors, in your role as a change practitioner you will wear many hats. These hats or skill sets serve different but related purposes and compliment each other.

■ *Analyzing and Designing Hat*
The hat for analyzing issues and designing appropriate solutions represents foundation skills:

● thinking analytically
● thinking "out-of-the box"
● learning continuously
● creating solutions

These skills allow you, through tactics like surveys, focus groups, observation, and data collection to see and design the best solution fit for change-related problems. It helps to develop and make use of instruments like the *Performance/Issue Analysis* sidebar and the *Change Management Planning* job aid (parts I and II) to achieve this. These types of tools help you ask the right questions and organize the information in a way that creates a visual framework of the problem.

■ *Strategy Hat*
Seeing the big picture, thinking holistically, and responding to clients are important when deciding what broad strategies to use in the change plan. It is simply a matter of identifying factors in

the business, economic, political, and social environment (like those shown in the sidebar at left). You must also realize that customer demands drive the need for change and dictate the required response to it.

■ *Change Agent Hat*
Everyone in the organization is in essence a change agent. Change management is not one department or one person; therefore, building a network of advocates and champions is critical. You should not underestimate the value of good press or word of mouth advertising. It creates needed momentum. To create that momentum, skills such as using human-relations techniques, creating partnerships, and leveraging influence are desirable for your change management role.

■ *Technology and Leadership Hat*
Using technology and project leadership methods are two skills that can prove to be your best friends in fostering change. Technology can support creative change programs or solutions, such as performance coaching through video-conferencing or virtual brainstorming using bulletin boards on an intranet.

Virtual brainstorming is a creative way to foster idea sharing across geographic and department boundaries because there is not always the opportunity to meet in person. It can also foster involvement and network building. The actual brainstorming process would involve posting questions or needs on the intranet bulletin board. Employees would place responses to questions or needs (adding to each other's ideas) on the board either independently (that is, asynchronous postings) or employees would be on-line at the same time for a designated period (that is, a synchronous chat). The responses could be in narrative form, lists, or even mind maps. Creativity would be the key and visual images (words or pictures) stimulate creativity. The responses would remain on the intranet as information resources.

Finally, in your change management role you will orchestrate a number of wide-ranging activities such as the following:

● breaking large tasks down into specific activities
● ensuring adequate time for those activities
● conducting a cost analysis

Big Picture/Holistic View

External Environment
● competitors
● government regulations
● societal changes (for example demographic shifts)
● globalization
● expanding technology
● decreasing product appeal
● growing niche markets
● politics

Internal Environment
● formal and informal communication
● financial picture
● decision making
● rewards
● predominate leadership style
● selection and promotion
● training and development
● performance measurement and feedback

Performance/Issue Analysis

Use the performance/issue analysis tool to map out a problem from a holistic viewpoint. It will help you to determine what systems or processes in the organization have an impact on the problem and to what degree. This process is key to ensuring that you identify the real causes of the problem and understand the full affect of those causes.

Date: **Change Consultant:**   **Client:**   **Problem Category:**

Stakeholders	**Process** What are the processes involved in the performance issue— jobs, roles, tasks, procedures, and so forth?	**People/Departments** Who are the people or departments affected by the performance issue?	**Picture of Ideal Environment** What would things look like if the problem did not exist? 1._____ 2._____ 3._____	**Value** What value does fixing the problem add to the bottom line?

Organizational Systems and Processes	Lack of Solution Fit (Y/N)	Degree (high, medium, low)	Relationship to Problem/Issue
Communication			
Training and Development			
Rewards and Recognition			
Performance Management			
Selection and Promotion			
Customer Input			
Employee Involvement			

© 1997, S. Cowan

Change Management Tactics

A dictionary might define "tactics" as maneuvers, procedures, or schemes—and all three apply within the context of change management. Tactics are the individual actions you use to ignite, maintain, and revitalize (if necessary) the change process. Listed below are some sample tactics you might consider using in your change efforts.

Meetings
- all-employee meetings—scheduled on a regular basis or as needed
- leadership meetings—scheduled on a regular basis or as needed
- quick focus sessions (for example, lesson-learned session after project completion or team intervention)
- department huddles (that is, impromptu, informal department gatherings for giving information, celebrating, or reinforcing morale)

Telephone Coaching
- performance, career, or process coaches can use
- potential coaches include human resources (HR) staff, internal subject matter experts (SMEs), and external consultant experts

On-Site Coaching
- performance, career, and process coaches can use this tactic with groups or individuals
- potential coaches include HR staff, internal SMEs, and external consultant experts

Communication Vehicles
- newsletters
- department bulletin boards
- intranet bulletin boards
- all-employee letters

Telephone Hot Line
- employees submit questions, share challenges and successes, and request information

Training
- classroom, on-the-job, or self-instructional (for example, workbook, video, CD-ROM-based) training for technical or behavioral issues
- knowledge/information partnerships
- learning contracts
- action plan for transferring learning
- peer teaching

Tools and Models
- help develop skills transfer knowledge and provide a means for applying learning (for example, a communication debrief and the *Four Point Coaching Model* presented on page 11)

Nerve Center
- group containing key personnel, technology, and resources for deploying and coordinating change leadership tactics across the organization

Survival Kit
- application-oriented tips and resources for coping through an organizational change

Recognition Day/Week
- leadership and co-worker acknowledgement of employee contribution
- banners, certificates, and profiles in the organization's newsletter recognizing achievements
- non-monetary rewards such as flextime, compressed workweek, special assignment, resources or technology, and special partnerships

Being able to manage these types of activities well is why project leadership skills are beneficial in a change management position.

Operationalizing the Change Strategy

The change management strategy starts from the big picture view, which is very broad and incorporates a number of initiatives. Operationalizing the strategy simply means breaking down the broad and wide into action-oriented activities (for example, programs, processes, or events) that move the change forward. The change practitioner can embrace these activities and measure progress and success easier.

While all of the tactics listed in the above sidebar are effective in facilitating change, a few deserve some additional attention:

- tools and models
- training and coaching

Tools and Models

The organization's employees are the bedrock of successful change tactics. As harbingers of the new culture, they must believe in the vision and use job behaviors that support realization of it. Obviously, changing performance or job behavior is not an exact science. It requires, among other factors, a way to perform the following:

- create common practices
- communicate those practices
- support application of those practices

One such way is developing or adopting appropriate performance tools and models. A performance tool is a logical, straightforward learning or application aid (such as the *Communications Debrief* on the following page). A performance model is a succinct, easily applied example of a process or procedure (see the *Four Point Coaching Model* sidebar on page 57 for an example and design tips).

Both models and tools provide a mental picture, which provide a more assessable framework for analysis or discussion. They also present a structured way of digesting information and perform the triple duty of teaching, coaching, and reinforcing.

Teaching. The boxes in the *Four Point Coaching Model*—observe, individualize, encourage, and track—represent separate subject areas for training in the classroom. Organize activities or exercises around each area. You can also design each area as a mini, stand-alone training module (possibly 45-90 minutes).

Coaching. Use the coaching questions on the Communication Debrief to guide discussion, identify challenges, and determine development needs during individual coaching sessions.

Reinforcing. The call-outs in the Communication Debrief make it easy to review and reinforce the application tips.

The idea is to pass the knowledge along while creating a sense of independence. This act builds the change tactics infrastructure, which is an important part of transforming the culture.

Training and Coaching

Training and coaching are interrelated essential parts of the infrastructure. With the redesign of jobs, the reengineering of whole processes, and the introduction of new technology, a need definitely exists for training employees. Training can occur in the classroom or on the job, but it also includes self-instructional training and performance coaching. No matter how you decide to provide it, training should be *application-oriented*. This means that the instructional strategy focuses on how to apply the classroom concepts on the job.

To ensure that training transfers to on-the-job application, include a process and worksheets on application planning in your training programs. Design your instruction to place less emphasis on conveying concepts and more emphasis on creating experiential learning opportunities (for example, simulations, role plays, learning games, and behavior modeling).

The *Leader as Change Facilitator* sidebar on page 59 is an example of an application-oriented program. The theme of the program is "Be a change *instigator* not a change *spectator*." A segment from W. Mitchell's powerful book *It's Not What Happens to You, It's What You Do About It* is included as pre-reading. The program is a one and a half-day classroom experience with follow-up coaching for the implementation activities. A pre-training survey is administered (preferably in person) to gather the following information from the leader:

- department's key customers
- methods for collecting customer data
- methods for communicating with staff

Both the survey and follow-up coaching, which can be in person, by telephone, or by e-mail, help establish a partnership between you and your customers. Through activities like these you increase your sensitivity to your customers' world (that is, their requirements, issues, and challenges).

Communication Debrief

Below is a sample of a communication debrief, which is a leader development tool. Use it as an example of how to learn from your meeting experience.

Briefly summarize the results of the meeting.

Base the debrief checklist on your task actions and use it to help you reflect on the way you conducted the meeting.

Whether or not you need to obtain information from the person depends on the nature of the meeting.

Action: Something you did—like not refocusing the group when it went on a tangent in the middle of the meeting. Unchecked tangents can kill the momentum and consume valuable time.

Statement: Something you said such as, "Ron, it's silly to feel anxious about the new job roles." Minimizing how someone feels makes that person defensive and less open to the message or purpose of the meeting.

Not all meetings require actions, resources, or deadlines as outcomes. For those that do, try to involve the group members (that is, solicit their input and ideas) in developing these items. When people are involved they are more receptive and feel ownership of the outcomes.

Date:	Communication Topic:	
How did the meeting go overall?	**What action or statement would I repeat? Why was the action or statement effective?**	**What action or statement would I *not* repeat?** **Why was the action or statement ineffective? How would I change it?**
Debrief Checklist		
☐ Did I begin by describing the **purpose** (for example, communicate a new policy) and desired **outcome?**		
☐ Did I **address questions** or concerns about the purpose or outcome (for example, whether or not the new policy being communicated would also be provided in writing)?		
☐ Did I **obtain information** needed to meet the purpose?		
☐ Did I **provide clarity** or background information on issues related to the purpose (for example, the criteria used to make a policy decision)?		
☐ Did I **deliver the complete message** or information? Did I verify whether the group understood the message?		
☐ Did I develop **next actions** (if required), with input from the group?		
☐ Did I identify **resources,** with input from the group?		
☐ Did I set **deadlines** for completion of actions, with input from the group?		
☐ Did I **restate** the outcomes at the end of the meeting?		
☐ Did I **check for unanswered questions** or concerns before concluding? Did I answer or make arrangements to get answers to the group later?		
☐ Did I **thank the group** for participating in the meeting?		

Four Point Coaching Model

Observe and respond to coaching opportunities.

● Pay attention to behaviors, actions, and feedback that indicate a need for coaching (for example, customer or peer complaints, procrastination, or expression of uncertainty about handling project).

Track performance and provide feedback.

● Reinforce desired performance.

● Identify ineffective performance and suggest alternative actions.

Individualize the coaching style based on who is being coached and the particular circumstances of the coaching opportunity.

● Consider the person's abilities, experience, willingness, work style, and confidence level—*the who*.

● Consider the deadline, resources, complexity of the task, impact of the task, logistics, organizational priority, and so forth—*the circumstances*.

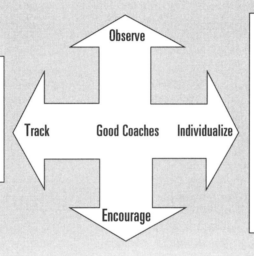

Encourage initiative and ownership, and offer support and guidance.

● Ask open-ended question to solicit input such as ideas, actions, and solutions.

● Provide expertise, experience, knowledge, and direction.

● Balance the "asking" and the "providing."

© July 1998, S. Cowan.

Implementation Roadblocks

Just because senior leadership has decided that the organization needs to change, it does not mean automatic success. Implementation roadblocks manifest themselves in many ways. No matter how well designed your overall strategy is or how skilled you are—you will likely confront some of the following roadblocks.

Lack of vision. When the corporate vision or specific business strategies are unclear, people are sometimes unsure about how they should interpret changes.

Lack of leadership support. The change manager is often the chief advocate of the change process. This role includes injecting the sense of advocacy into the rest of the organization—particularly leadership. Actions that are essential for success must first be present in leaders. They must model the behaviors needed to bring about change in both process and culture. Only top leadership can provide the sanctions of time and resources necessary for change. They must also remove obstacles to change that are out of the realm of direct reports. Problems occur when senior leadership says one thing, but their behaviors suggest the opposite.

Lack of HR systems alignment. Hiring people with the right abilities and attitude, rewarding people for the right behaviors and outputs, and training people in the right skills are all part of aligning the systems to provide what you need to redesigned the culture.

History of poor implementation. When an organization has a history of poorly implemented strategic plans, people tend to expect very little when new change efforts are announced.

Insufficient time. If insufficient time is allocated for implementation, there will be large maintenance cost after the change.

Environment of low risk taking. Overly punishing errors or rewarding the mere absence of errors promotes an environment of low risk taking. High risk taking should be the desired behavior in an organization undergoing change.

Lack of clear communications. If information about change is allowed to filter down the organization in an unmanaged fashion, it becomes diffused, less specific, and interpreted in arbitrary ways.

Lack of resistance planning. All major changes, even ones that have positive implications, encounter resistance. People are not necessarily resisting change but rather the disruption caused by change.

Poor management of resistance. When resistance does not surface, it is often because it has been denied or quashed. When overt resistance is not acknowledged and managed properly, the resistance often goes "underground." The results are covert resistance:

- slowdowns
- malicious compliance
- outright sabotage

Lack of synergy. Forgetting that an organization's various operations are interdependent can lead to initiating changes in one place and encountering resistance from people and functions in another place.

Poor follow-through. Many organizations reward people with a lot of fanfare for starting big projects, but they fail to follow-through to see that the project was finished or that it achieved the desired results.

Roadblocks like these just prove that the world of change management is unpredictable, exciting, and challenging. During change, addressing both the process needs *and* the people needs of your organization is a complex—but necessary—balancing act.

As the change manager, you and the committed, visible support of top leadership are the primary catalysts of this balancing act. Your ability to translate broad strategy into action-oriented tactics lays a pathway for creating real systems and behavioral change. Moreover, thriving on the excitement, enduring the challenges, and expecting the unpredictability are the hallmarks of a successful change manager.

Leader as Change Facilitator

Below is an example of the course design for an application-oriented program. The theme for this program was "Be a change *instigator* not a change *spectator*." Use this example to help you design your own application-oriented programs that facilitate change.

Section	Title	Content
Introduction/ Ice Breaker	**Change is like …**	Ask participants to stand beneath one of the four flipchart titles (listed below) that best describes their feelings about change. ● Change is like a roller coaster ride—*It is both exhilarating and frightening.* ● Change is like a new pair of shoes—*It is tight and uncomfortable until you break it in.* ● Change is like a hot fudge sundae—*It is delicious and satisfying and leaves you eagerly anticipating the next one.* ● Change is like a hailstorm—*It is fast and furious and you just have to ride it out.* Once participants are gathered beneath the flipcharts, ask them to chat for a minute about their reaction to recent changes in their lives. Next, ask them one-by-one to introduce themselves (for example, name, department, job/responsibility, and reason they stood beneath that particular flipchart) to the large group.
Opening Activity	**What, why, and how**	Through use of poster boards, summary information sheets, question and answer time, and an appearance from someone in senior leadership, address the following questions: ● What is changing? ● Why is it changing? ● How will it benefit the organization? ● How can it benefit the organization's employees?
Learning Outcomes	**Goals**	Asking these questions is critical in setting a framework for the learning and application process. Discuss the fact that a certain amount of ambiguity comes with dramatic organizational change—not all questions can be answered. ● Understand change in general. ● Understand implications of the change or transition for the organization. ● Understand leader's role in facilitating change or transition. ● Develop a plan for helping staff manage change or transition.
Department Environment Maps		Through an interactive exercise using the department environment maps that were created during pre-training sessions, participants should realize the following: ● They have similar challenges. ● They share customers, technology, and resources. ● They have common goals. ● They can be a resource to each other.
Supervisor's or Manager's Role	**Change— personal view**	Examine the personal view of change through an activity involving a three-part instrument: ● change grid (What does change look like? How does it affect me?) ● change pulse (How do I feel about the change? Where am I on the change Adaptation/Acceptance Spectrum?) ● change implementation (What can I do to adapt/accept this change? What can I do to facilitate the change?)
Management Behaviors	**Eight keys**	Examine the eight keys of management leadership (listed below), and, using an assessment process, determine development needs relative to the eight keys: ● listening ● collaborating ● recognizing/rewarding ● presenting information ● communicating one-on-one ● coaching ● supporting ● clearing the way
Action Planning		Complete a plan for transferring the learning to the job (for example, what will be done, when, who needs to be involved, resources, benefits, and so forth). The training department sets up a coaching schedule for continued support during implementation.

© *July 1998, S. Cowan.*

References & Resources

Articles

Barrier, Michael. "Managing Workers in a Time of Change." *Nation's Business.* May 1998, pp. 31-34.

Buchel, Mary. "Accelerating Change." *Training & Development.* April 1996, pp. 48-51.

Carrig, Ken. "Reshaping Human Resources for the Next Century—Lessons from a High Flying Airline." *Human Resource Management.* Summer 1997, pp. 277-289.

Caudron, Shari. "Rebuilding Employee Trust." *Training & Development.* August 1996, pp. 18-21.

Cook, Julie. "Tackling Large-Scale Change." *Human Resource Executive.* May 20, 1997, pp. 44-46.

Cutcher-Gershenfeld, Joel, et al. "Managing Concurrent Change Initiatives: Integrating Quality and Work/Family Strategies." *Organizational Dynamics.* Winter 1997, pp. 21-37.

Demers, Russ, et al. "Commitment to Change." *Training & Development.* August 1996, pp. 22-26.

Denton, D. Keith. "9 Ways to Create an Atmosphere for Change." *HRMagazine.* October 1996, pp. 76-81.

Frady, Marsha. "Get Personal to Communicate Coming Change." *Performance Improvement.* August 1997, pp. 32-33.

Kramlinger, Tom. "How to Deliver a Change Message." *Training & Development.* April 1998, pp. 44-47.

Orlikowski, Wanda J., and Debra J. Hofman. "An Improvisational Model for Change Management: the Case of Groupware Technologies." *Sloan Management Review.* Winter 1997, pp. 11-21.

Prickett, Ruth. "House Proud." *People Management.* November 12, 1998, pp. 43-45.

Rough, Jim. "Dynamic Facilitation and the Magic of Self-Organizing Change." *Journal for Quality and Participation.* June 1997, pp. 34-38.

Schneider, David M., and Charles Goldwasser. "Be a Model Leader of Change." *Management Review.* March 1998, pp. 41-45.

Smith, Dick. "Invigorating Change Initiatives." *Management Review.* May 1998, pp. 45-48.

Strebel, Paul. "Why Do Employees Resist Change?" *Harvard Business Review.* May/June 1996, pp. 86-92.

Topchik, Gary S. "Attacking the Negativity Virus." *Management Review.* September 1998, pp. 61-64.

Trahant, Bill, and Warner W. Burke. "Traveling Through Transitions." *Training & Development.* February 1996, 37-41.

Books

Barger, Nancy J., and Linda K. Kirby. *The Challenge of Change in Organizations: Helping Employees Thrive in the New Frontier.* Palo Alto, CA: Davies-Black, 1995.

Carr, Clay. *Choice, Change & Organizational Change: Practical Insights from Evolution for Business Leaders & Thinkers.* New York: AMACOM, 1996.

Hambrick, Donald C., et al. (eds.) *Navigating Change: How CEOs, Top Teams, and Boards Steer Transformation.* Boston: Harvard Business School Press, 1998.

Jeffreys, J. Shep. *Coping with Workplace Change: Dealing with Loss and Grief.* Menlo Park, CA: Crisp Publications, 1995.

Maurer, Rick. *Beyond the Wall of Resistance: Unconventional Strategies that Build Support for Change.* Austin, TX: Bard Books, 1996.

Mitchell, W. *It's Not What Happens to You, It's What You Do About It.* Partners Publishers Group, 1997.

Smith, Douglas K. *Taking Charge of Change: 10 Principles for Managing People and Performance.* Reading, MA: Addison-Wesley, 1996.

Info-lines

Carr, Don Aaron. "How to Facilitate." No. 9406 (revised 1999).

Koehle, Deborah. "The Role of the Performance Change Manager." No. 9715.

Smith, Warren. "Managing Change: Implementation Skills." No. 8910 (out of print).

Titcomb, T. J. "Chaos and Complexity Theory." No. 9807.

Change Management Planning

This job aid has two parts. Part I provides descriptions of when particular change tactics are most appropriate. Part II provides space for you to list the various components of your program and to select the change management tactics you think best support each component. The purpose of the descriptions and the worksheet is to support designing the best overall strategy for a specific change-related problem.

Part I.

Tact	Application
Education	Appropriate when looking to close a **knowledge gap** or **skill deficiency** that requires college or technical education (such as the completion of a degree or certificate).
Training	Applies when **job processes** or **job technologies** have changed and internal training programs are available to meet the need. Local colleges and training firms offer technical, skills, and interpersonal training.
Coaching/ Counseling	There are four types of coaching or counseling: ● **Performance coaching** closes gaps in the quality or production of an individual's or a group's work outputs. It can involve reviewing examples of desired outputs, reinforcing strategies for producing desired outputs, and giving constructive feedback on outputs. ● **Career coaching** is useful during workforce transition situations (such as job transfer, elimination, or redesign). It can involve skills assessment, resume writing, cover letter writing, job searching tips (internal or external), and education planning. ● **Process coaching** supports groups working on their flow-charting of processes, identifying redundancies, and recommending improvements or changes. It is also an appropriate analysis activity when reengineering organizational systems. ● **Human relations coaching** provides support, insight, or guidance in handling inter-group or team relations, change adaptability, or communication issues.
Interviewing	Useful if you are collecting sensitive information, if the questions are mainly open-ended and less suited for a written survey, or if there is a need for the interviewer to interact with the interviewee during the interview. Can be done in-person or by telephone. In-person is desirable when hearing the information and seeing the person providing the information is beneficial to the outcome (for example, better opportunity to establish rapport or build relations and to observe the interviewee's behavior).
Mentoring Program	Useful if you want to **impart leadership knowledge** and **experience** to the culture. Appropriate for addressing **diversity issues** around change by establishing special programs for underrepresented groups. Can be an informal or formal program.
Tool or Model	Helpful in situations where a **job aid** can contribute to improving performance or can provide support in applying a process. Can supplement for formal training, be used as a guide when coaching, and is an effective method for enabling employees to perform independently.
Intervention	Involves using activities (such as team building, role clarification, or structured feedback) to influence behavior, stop certain behaviors, or increase awareness. The goal is to get a group back on track and can involve one activity or a series of activities designed to meet a specific need.
Assessment or Survey	Aids with **collecting employees' opinions** or **attitudes** about change (for example, change readiness survey or team participation survey).
Focus Group	Useful to **obtain sensitive information,** debrief after an incident to channel emotions, debrief after completion of a project for lessons learned, or assess employees' readiness for or adaptation to change. Can be intact or cross-functional groups.
Communi- cation	Used to inform, educate, motivate, or influence. Newsletters, e-mail, voice-mail, all-employee letters, banners, and bulletin boards are examples of communication vehicles. Appropriate during change (for example, a merger) because **employees need and want to be informed** of what is happening and motivated to stay engaged. A communication vacuum leads to half-truths, innuendoes, and lies. Communication during all phases of change is necessary. Timeliness, honesty, and consistency are key.

Job Aid

Action Planning	Helpful in transferring classroom learning to the job, applying a process to a situation, and implementing individual or group performance development activities.
System Alignment	Involves changing systems (such as compensation, performance review, training, and selection/promotion) to support the type of culture the organization wants to build. For example, if your organization wants to create a culture of entrepreneurial thinkers, the design of its compensation system might include a reward (such as a bonus) for developing and successfully implementing ideas that grow the business. Elements like employee empowerment, risk-taking, and trust would have to be a part of this culture. You would also need an infrastructure of resources, tracking methods, and reporting. (This is actually more of a strategy than a tactic.)

Part II.

	Appropriate Change Management Tactic					
Project Components	Education	Training	Coaching/ Counseling	Interviewing	Mentoring Programs	Tool or Model

Project Components	Intervention	Assessment or Survey	Focus Group	Communi- cation	Action Planning	System Alignment

16 Steps To Becoming
A Learning Organization

Issue 9602

16 Steps To Becoming A Learning Organization

AUTHOR:

Dr. Michael Marquardt
President, Global Learning Associates
1688 Moorings Drive
Reston, VA 22090
Tel. 703/437-2060
FAX: 703/437-3725

Michael Marquardt is a professor of HRD at George Washington University and President of Global Learning Associates, an organization that assists corporations and public agencies in becoming learning organizations. He is the author of more than 50 books and articles.

Editorial staff for 9602

Editor
Warren Shaver, Jr.

ASTD Internal Consultant
Michele Brock

Revised 1997

Editor
Cat Sharpe

Associate Editor
Patrick McHugh

Designer
Steven M. Blackwood

The Starting Line

Things move faster every day. To keep up, we must stay on our toes and adapt, change, and learn at every opportunity. Every day. All the time.

And we are not alone. Organizational entities—from entrepreneurial start-ups to international megacorporations—also must find ways to learn continuously or they too will be left at the station. Becoming a learning organization is one surefire way to stay on track, on time, and ahead of the competition.

We can think of most organizational strategies as roads that lead to some destination. For example, we may want to reengineer a process to increase productivity. Once that process is fixed, the initiative is over. Even if we continuously improve the process, we can see that this action is a series of single initiatives—small journeys with defined destinations.

In a learning organization, the journey never ends. Initiatives such as continuous process improvement are just part of a learning organization's overall goal: for everyone in the company to learn as much and as often as possible to increase productivity. Specifically, this means that learning organizations practice and improve the skills and principles of learning throughout the organization as well as up and down the business chain.

This *Info-line* will define one learning organization model, present real-world examples of learning organizations at work, and give you 16 steps your organization can take to begin its journey.

Becoming a Learning Organization

There is no single, guaranteed way to become a learning organization. Each organization must look at its own history, competitive environment, skill base, technology, mission, and culture and then develop an appropriate learning structure and style. Or, using the journey metaphor above, the organization must decide where the path is headed and then figure out how to walk.

Despite differences in specific techniques, all learning organizations use five interrelated systems to build their learning paths: the organization itself, its people, its technology, its knowledge, and its overall learning. (The sidebar on the following two pages explains these systems in detail.) Getting all these systems to work—and work well together—is not easy. But there is no more important task to ensure the survival and success of a learning organization.

We also must understand that a true learning organization never stops becoming a learning organization. The process does not end because change does not end. The need for learning will always exist.

Even with these caveats in mind, we can still create clear guidelines for companies that want to begin this journey. The best directions come from other learning organizations. If we analyze the strategies and steps these successful companies have taken, we can see that they didn't just happen to become learning organizations. They planned for and committed themselves to the concept of continuous, organization-wide learning, and they continue to exhibit patterns of behavior and action that other organizations can consider, modify, and perform.

The following 16 steps consolidate and condense these patterns. As you review each step, think about the following questions:

● Does your organization follow this step? If not, could it?

● What would it take for your organization to complete this step or to follow it better? What barriers exist that might prevent your organization from following this step?

● What could you do to help your organization follow this step? What barriers exist that might prevent you from acting on this step?

What Is a Learning Organization?

The Description

In general, learning organizations will possess such characteristics as those listed below. Each of these characteristics are part and parcel of the systems model in the next section.

- The organizational system learns as a whole, almost as if the organization were a single brain.

- People in the organization recognize that ongoing, organization-wide learning is critical for the organization's current as well as future success.

- Learning is a continuous, strategically used process that is integrated with and parallel to work.

- Focus is on creativity and generative learning.

- Belief is that systems thinking is fundamental.

- People have continuous access to information and data resources important to the company's success.

- The organizational climate encourages, rewards, and accelerates individual and group learning.

- Workers are innovative and communal in their networking, both inside and outside the organization.

- The organization embraces change, and views unexpected surprises and failures as opportunities to learn.

- The organization is agile and flexible.

- People in the organization are driven by a desire for quality and continuous improvement.

- Aspiration, reflection, and conceptualization characterize most organizational activities.

- Well-developed core competencies serve as the launching points for new products and services.

- The organization can continuously adapt, renew, and revitalize itself in response to changing environments.

The Systems Model

In the systems model of the learning organization, the organization is a system with five interrelated components: the learning, the organization, the people, the knowledge, and the technology.

■ *Learning*

The core component of this model is learning. In a learning organization, the learning is continuous and conscious. It thoroughly permeates the other four components, just as these components enhance and augment the learning's quality and effect.

Learning should also happen at three different levels: individual, group or team, and organizational. All three types of learning depend on sharing knowledge and past experience. Companies must use their organizational "brains"—that is, their policies, strategies, and explicit models—to do this.

In addition, Peter Senge, in his book *The Fifth Discipline,* has identified six skills—or disciplines—that affect learning in an organization:

1. Systems thinking—a conceptual framework that makes patterns (and ways to change them) more understandable.

2. Mental models—deeply ingrained assumptions that influence how we understand and take action in the world.

3. Personal mastery—proficiency in a subject or skill.

4. Team learning—the process of developing a team that learns and produces.

5. Shared vision—finding common ground in an organization that fosters real commitment, rather than simple compliance

6. Dialogue—the free and creative exploration of subtle issues, a deep listening to others, and the suspension of one's own views.

The Organization

The organizational component creates and fosters powerful and productive ways to learn throughout the organization. It can do this in four ways:

1. Culture—the values, beliefs, customs, and practices of an organization. In a learning organization, the culture realizes that learning is essential for a successful business, has made learning a habit, and has integrated learning into all organizational functions.

2. Vision—the organization's goals and direction for the future. In a learning organization, the desired future is one in which learners create better and better products and services.

3. Strategy—the tactics, methods, and action plans an organization uses to reach its goals. In a learning organization, these strategies improve the collection, transferal, and use of knowledge in all corporate actions.

4. Structure—the organization's configuration. In a learning organization, the structure is flat, boundaryless, and streamlined. It fosters contact, information flow, local responsibility, and collaboration.

The People

People—both inside and outside the learning organization—are empowered to learn whatever they need to know to improve productivity. Groups of people affected by the learning organization include:

- **Employees** must plan for future competencies, take action, and take risks.

- **Managers** must coach and mentor their employees, modeling good learning behaviors.

- **Customers** must identify needs and receive appropriate training in the organization's products and services.

- **The community** will both receive and provide knowledge from the learning organization as it ventures into the social and education arenas.

Knowledge

The learning organization will collect, create, store, transfer, and use knowledge effectively and productively. These elements are ongoing, interactive, and often simultaneous.

- **Collection.** The organization will seek and get knowledge from inside and outside the organization.

- **Creation.** The organization will create new knowledge through insight, problem solving, and experience.

- **Storage.** The organization will store valued knowledge so any staff member can access it anytime, from anywhere.

- **Transfer.** The organization will move information mechanically, electronically, and interpersonally.

- **Use.** Members of an organization, as well as the organization as a whole, will use the information and knowledge.

The Technology

The technology component of a learning organization is an organization's supporting and integrated electronic networks and tools. This includes the technical processes, systems, and structure of its knowledge freeway, such as:

Information technology—any electronic system that gathers, codes, stores, and transfers information across the organization and between organizations.

Technology-based learning—the delivery and sharing of knowledge and skills through video, audio, and computer-based multimedia training.

Electronic performance support systems (EPSS)—electronic tools that use multimedia knowledge bases to capture, store, and distribute information throughout an organization. They deliver information on the job, just in time, and with minimum staff support.

For more information on learning organizations, see *Info-line* No. 9306, "Learning Organizations: The Trainer's Role."

Adapted from Building the Learning Organization *by Michael Marquardt. Copyright 1996, McGraw-Hill. All rights reserved.*

■ *STEP 1: Commitment*

Most importantly, an organization's top leaders must be committed to transforming the company into a learning organization. Whether the impetus for change comes from a single charismatic leader or from a critical mass of managers, the leadership must understand and believe that business success depends on learning success. Specifically, they must recognize that only a learning organization can give customers the products and services they want and, therefore, that learning organizations generate the best long-term profits.

The reason for this is simple. A learning organization can rapidly transform its new knowledge into new products, new marketing strategies, and new ways of doing business. As an added benefit, a learning organization can be an exciting, enjoyable, and fulfilling place to work. Such an organization can employ top people, bringing even more learning to the company and further increasing productivity.

■ *STEP 2: Connection*

The leaders in a new learning organization have to connect clearly and explicitly link the processes and products of learning to the strategic goals of the organization. It is much easier to persuade people throughout the organization about the importance of this dramatic new direction by showing the direct connections between learning and improved business operations. Employees need to know that, although initial difficulties and challenges will arise, the eventual rewards will be worth the trouble.

One way to link learning with organizational strategy is to establish a learning team that advises, counsels, and reviews the overall direction of learning. This team ensures that learning fits and promotes the organization's strategic goals. Rover, a leading auto manufacturer in Great Britain, realized that the best way to get employees on the learning organization boat would be to define and achieve measurable benefits from learning. The company did this by forming Rover Learning Business, a separate corporate entity devoted to learning.

You can use the following points to help convince any doubters in your organization:

Learning is a task. In fact, it is as much an organizational task as is the production and delivery of goods and services. Productivity and profits are as important as ever; company-wide learning is the way to get them.

Learning can fit into daily operations. It must. Speed and quality need not be sacrificed in order to learn. In fact, employees should learn from their daily operations. Every activity-from planning, through execution, to assessment-is an occasion to learn. This type of "action learning" is critical to business success for many learning organizations, including General Electric and Motorola.

Learning stores organizational memory. Learning organizations can retain valuable business knowledge, even if individual employees leave. The reason for this is that the organization has developed comprehensive and systematic ways to capture valuable knowledge that previously may have been kept only in the minds of those employees.

■ *STEP 3: Assessment*

As in most change efforts, a critical early step is to assess the organization's existing strengths, weaknesses, and resources in all five systems of the learning organization. Although an organization can implement an informal assessment of its learning, it is better to examine comprehensively and systematically the organization's learning competence. Tools such as the Learning Organization Profile on pages 14-15 can help formalize your efforts.

■ *STEP 4: Communication*

Once an organization commits itself to the idea of learning, it must communicate this vision to all employees and stakeholders (including those outside the organization). When everyone has the same stars to steer by, people can better understand and enthusiastically support this new organizational vision. Other reasons to convey this vision strategically include:

● A vision gives employees—and the organization itself—an overarching goal and direction to help guide strategic thinking and planning.

- The loftiness of the target compels new ways of thinking and acting. It generates powerful and creative learning that leads to high quality products and services.

- A vision provides a rudder to keep the learning processes and efforts on course in the face of stress, frustration, and impatience.

- People can better accomplish tasks that fall within their own personal vision. Stating an organizational vision allows people to align this vision with their own.

Jim Gannon, vice-president of human resource planning and development for the Royal Bank of Canada, underscores the critical value of communicating the vision of corporate-wide learning: "Visions are what energize the organization; they are the dreams that pull us forward. The learning vision, like any vision, must be communicated effectively since even the most sophisticated vision is of no use unless it can be clearly understood by others."

■ STEP 5: Recognition

To build a learning organization, people in the company must recognize the importance of systems thinking and systems action—that is, to see patterns and opportunities, to focus on the interdependency of all parts of the organization, and to see problems and solutions in terms of systematic relationships.

Systems thinking will help people see patterns clearly and identify ways to change these patterns more effectively. Systems action lets people focus on high-level changes that may not be obvious—for example, starting a comprehensive orientation for new employees that lets them work better sooner. Together, these techniques help the organization begin its corporation-wide learning. For more information on systems thinking, see *Info-line* No. 9703, "Systems Thinking."

Companies such as Wal-Mart, Proctor & Gamble, and Cray have used systems thinking and systems action to encourage their workers to:

- Ask "why" something was a challenge, success, or failure.

Case Study: Learning at Rover

Rover realized that intensifying industrial competition throughout the world put an increasing premium on the company's ability to do more than satisfy suppliers and customers. The company had to "delight" them. This was particularly true in the fiercely competitive international motor industry.

Rover devotes significant resources to learning programs for dealers. Popular distance learning programs include a library of sales and after-sales skill improvement, product knowledge, and servicing techniques videos. In addition, service correspondence courses attract over 500 participants per year. And Rover offers tutored courses at its various facilities for interested dealer staff.

Recently, Rover launched a quality management program and customer service initiative. The program provides a structured career path, via a "learning and competence accreditation ladder." In its first year, over 2,000 dealer staff from over 500 dealerships enrolled in what has been described as a "remarkable confirmation of the continuous learning ethos" in Rover.

In a real learning organization coup, Rover also decided not only to learn about their suppliers, dealers, and customers, but to have them learn about Rover as well. The company began to offer courses to help suppliers meet the auto industry's demanding standards of quality and efficiency.

- Determine which high-leverage actions to take.

- Realize that cause and effect are not always closely related in time and space.

- Recognize and understand the links between actions.

- Create archetypes of successful actions for the organization to follow.

■ STEP 6: Demonstration and Modeling

Learning organizations need leaders to demonstrate their support and to model their commitment to learning. Leaders in a company—especially during the early stages of the learning organization—should have but one aim: to pursue improved performance by fostering long-term learning and continuous improvement. Being the champion of organizational learning should be seen as the responsibility of (and an opportunity for) every manager.

As top managers become convinced of the value of a learning organization, they must also become learners. They should see themselves as coaches, facilitators, and advocates who promote, encourage, and reinforce learning. The Arthur Andersen Company gives each of its new managers a small card that describes this new model for managers. Following this model, supervisors become coaches, people become continuous learners, and activities become learning opportunities.

Consider some of the following steps leaders can take to promote organizational learning and create a corporate culture for learning.

Provide opportunities. Let workers train for and practice organizational learning.

Realize people make mistakes. Support and encourage workers to overcome any fear or shame they may feel if they make errors. Set norms that legitimize errors made while in search of progress.

Coach and reward efforts. Set norms that reward innovative thinking and experimentation.

■ *STEP 7: Transformation*
Once people know what a learning organization is, and that the company wants to strive to become one, they need to start transforming the business culture to one of continual learning and improvement. Ongoing learning should become a work habit and an integral part of every business action, including production, marketing, problem solving, finance, customer service, and so on.

A driving force in all learning organizations is the commitment to continuous improvement, and organizations that practice total quality management (TQM) are already on the path toward corporation-wide learning. Why? Because one question is never far from the minds of everyone in such a company: "How can this be done better?" A continuous improvement culture is clearly a learning culture.

Motorola laid its foundation as a learning organization when the company made a commitment to the Six-Sigma Improvement Process that required that there be no more than 3.4 defects per million in manufactured goods. Reaching that goal—which Motorola has since exceeded—called for constant attention to improving every action and interaction in the organization. It forced Motorola to find ways to keep getting better. And that required people in the company to be learners and to help Motorola be a smarter organization.

If your organization's culture is not one of continuous improvement, take note of the following things the organization can do to start the transformation.

Provide opportunities for learning. Make learning events frequent and the environment safe and fun for learning.

Focus on continuous learning. Do this rather than holding one-time training events. The organization will eventually forge a new relationship with employees that demonstrates a belief in them and their ability to learn.

Make learning interesting. The organization can arrange events such as lectures, coffee klatches, panels, tours, videoconferences, and other types of regularly occurring programs. A varied and continual approach to learning helps keep employees interested in new ideas every day.

For more information on quality and continuous improvement, see *Info-line*s No. 9210, "Continuous Process Improvement," and No. 9111, "Fundamentals of Quality."

■ *STEP 8: Strategy*
Quantum leaps in learning cannot occur without corporate-wide strategies and tactics for expanding individual, team, and organizational levels of learning. Some of the most effective strategies include the following:

Encourage experimentation. Let people try new and different things. Provide time and rewards for innovations. Help people feel comfortable with and motivated toward experimentation.

Recognize and praise learners. Organizational heroes should be those who have stretched and experimented, who have tried and failed, who have learned a lot—not those who simply never "rocked the boat."

Reward learning. Develop reward systems that compensate the learner.

Spread the word about new learning. Use formal and informal staff gatherings to exchange information and share learning experiences. National Semiconductor, for example, holds annual events where teams present their best projects, experiments, and innovations. Other companies write case studies about their successes and failures and use these cases in meetings and training programs.

Apply the new learning. Real business leverage comes from applying new learning in different places throughout your organization. People need to use what others have learned, and organizations must free up and motivate their workers to act. One great motivation is rewarding those who can apply other people's insights or their own new ideas.

■ *STEP 9: Cut and Streamline*

Bureaucracy is the bane of any organization seeking to gain the power of learning. It kills the energy, creativity, and willingness to risk that are necessary for learning to bloom. Regulations and forms for every possible scenario choke off learning. Author Thomas Peters declares in *Thriving on Chaos* that a priority for all learning organizations is to "demolish" their bureaucracies.

Ways to streamline an organization include the following methods:

Reengineer. That is, eliminate any business processes that decrease learning, the flow of knowledge, or the empowering of employees.

Refocus. Build a structure around projects and customers rather than around traditional functional silos.

Decentralize. Put as much power at the point of action—and learning—as possible.

Clear out. Eliminate hard, bureaucratic structures and unnecessary policies and restrictions.

Eliminate. Get rid of vertical and horizontal barriers that stem the transfer of communications, ideas, and learning.

Introduce fluidity. Be able to reorganize—every day if necessary—to serve the needs of the marketplace. Build this capability into the organizational structure.

Bond. Weld all former functional activities into a seamless whole.

Organizations might also consider following the Royal Bank of Canada's lead. It encourages its workers to eliminate bureaucracy by challenging unnecessary forms and silly rules, ending systems and processes that discourage learning, and rewarding those actions that promote increasing knowledge and improving quality and service.

■ *STEP 10: Empower and Enable*

Empowered employees have the necessary freedom, trust, influence, opportunity, recognition, and authority to do their jobs. Enabled employees have the necessary skills, knowledge, values, and ability to do their jobs. Workers such as these are more comfortable following the vision and hopes of the company because they feel that they have a role to play in the organization's success and the skills needed to carry out this role.

Learning organizations recognize that empowered and enabled employees are essential for success. As Judith Vogt and Kenneth Murrell wrote in their book *Empowerment in Organizations*, empowerment is critical in a successful learning environment because it "sparks exceptional learning and performance." Organizations, therefore, need to free the worker to serve the customer. They must put decision-making power and accountability at the level closest to the action. And they should give the worker permission to spend money and cross functional borders in the pursuit of learning excellence.

Case Study: McKinsey & Company

All too often, valuable learning experiences, whether they come from successes or heart-wrenching failures, never leave the minds of the involved people or groups. Learning organizations know how to capture this learning through a variety of positive- and sometimes punitive-methods. Consider some of the following strategies used by global consulting giant McKinsey & Company Inc., one of the best knowledge management companies in the world.

- A director of knowledge management coordinates company efforts in creating and collecting knowledge.

- Knowledge transfer is a professional responsibility and part of everyone's job.

- Knowledge development is part of the personnel evaluation process.

- Employees must prepare a two-page summary of how and what they have learned from a project before they get a billing code.

- Every three months, each project manager receives a printout of what has been put into the company's information system.

- An online information system called the Practice Development Network is updated weekly and now has over 6,000 documents, including the *Knowledge Resource Directory*, a guide to who knows what in the company.

- For any of the 31 practice areas of McKinsey, an employee can find the list of its members, experts, and core documents by tapping into that firm's data base.

- A McKinsey *Bulletin* for one of the practice areas appears two or three times per week. They feature new ideas and information that the practice area wants to "parade" before the whole company.

The learning organization itself should use its time, money, and effort to help increase workers' skills. In fact, some companies spend over 5 percent of payroll for learning programs. The goal of such an organization is to get employees ready for their present jobs as well as for any unforeseen future challenges. These companies want their employees fully "informated" with financial, technical, and other kinds of data that will help them take the initiative and be proactive in their jobs.

For more information on empowerment, see *Info-line* No. 9105, "Basics of Employee Empowerment."

■ *STEP 11: Extend*

For learning organizations to truly tap into all their potential sources for knowledge and ideas, they must extend their learning efforts to all stakeholders, including customers, vendors, suppliers, and even the community around them. All these groups have a vested interest in the outcomes of the organization's learning and therefore can assist in validating needs analyses, learning goals, the design of learning packages, and the link between learning and business goals. Learning organizations should schedule and provide learning activities for these groups in ways that fit the schedules and learning styles of the stakeholders.

■ *STEP 12: Capture and Release*

People at every level of a learning organization will be challenged to develop new knowledge, to take responsibility for their new ideas, and to pursue these ideas as far as they can. The key challenge of a manager is to create an environment that allows workers to accomplish these goals.

Capture Learning

The capture of learning is the structured and continual collection of an organization's intelligence and knowledge. A learning organization should provide an array of opportunities and situations for its workers to capture learning, ranging from regular meetings and information exchanges to technological solutions such as central databases and e-mail.

Case Study: FedEx and EPSS

FedEx's customer service representatives get thousands of telephone calls a day, each of which demands ready answers. In the past, FedEx representatives handled questions by passing customers' calls to other, specialized representatives. An EPSS, however, now enables FedEx to resolve problems "immediately and proactively without passing off any customers," according to Bart Dahmer, manager of technology services and technical training at FedEx in Memphis, Tennessee.

This EPSS makes it possible for the customer service representatives to access one computer application without closing another. For example, representatives will not have to exit a "billing" application to get into the "customer service" application. They will be able to retrieve information from several databases at one time to address customers' specific problems, no matter how complex.

The system also prompts representatives while they are helping customers. For example, it cues representatives to give callers instructions on how to measure a box of any shape.

FedEx recently began a mandatory performance improvement program for all of its employees who deal with customers. The primary goals: to completely centralize the development of training content while decentralizing delivery and to audit the employees' ability to retain what they have learned.

The program consists of job knowledge tests that are linked to an interactive video instruction training curriculum on workstations in more than 700 locations nationwide. More than 35,000 FedEx customer-contact employees around the country are required to take the job knowledge tests annually at their work locations. The tests measure employees' knowledge in their specific jobs and correspond with employees' annual evaluations. The results of the tests make up approximately one-tenth of the employees' performance ratings.

By testing customer-contact employees on product knowledge services, policies, and various aspects of their jobs, FedEx obtains two major benefits, according to William Wilson, manager of training and testing technology.

1. All employees operate from the same book. This ensures that all customers will receive accurate and consistent information during every transaction, helping the company maintain its high level of service and commitment to quality.

2. Managers have an objective way to measure job knowledge for all customer-contact employees.

FedEx also provides incentives for workers to increase their learning in this program. For example, employees are paid for two hours of test preparation time, two hours of test time, and two hours of posttest study time.

The average amount of time that workers use the interactive video instruction program is approximately 132,000 hours per year. Compared to traditional training, this equates to approximately 800 one-day classes for 20 employees per class.

One facet of capturing learning is the learning audit. This audit measures organizational structures, time, and other resources to see how well the organization can create, enhance, and capture learning. Methods to link new learning to organizational productivity are carefully assessed and applied. The goal of a learning audit is to improve the ways an organization learns. In a way, it is the TQM process for learning itself.

Release Knowledge

If knowledge is power, then the release of knowledge is the release of power. Whether from person to person or from computer to person, such a release is an infusion of energy and strength into an organization. This is what learning organizations thrive on.

Learning Points

Most importantly, learning organizations realize that company-wide learning is crucial for continued success. Therefore, they focus efforts on corporate agility and flexibility, continuous improvement, and encouragement of learning among all of their employees.

There are various models of learning organizations. One focuses on five interrelated components: the organization, the people, the knowledge, the technology, and the learning.

The organizational learning component is responsible for creating and fostering new and productive ways for everyone to learn throughout the organization.

People inside and outside the organization are empowered to take risks, communicate, and learn so as to improve productivity.

The learning organization will collect, create, store, transfer, and use knowledge effectively and productively.

A learning organization will use an integrated network of electronic tools to capture, code, store, and distribute knowledge.

The learning component thoroughly permeates the other four components at three different levels: individual, group or team, and organizational.

However, this knowledge must move freely, easily, and quickly. If an organization sits on what it knows, its knowledge may become misinformation. Likewise, workers should be encouraged and trained to release their own knowledge and tap into that of others.

Note that knowledge needs to flow upward as well as downward through an organization for it to be truly helpful. The organization should host lots of open discussions. For example, consider the "lessons learned" meetings held regularly at the Nuclear Regulatory Commission. There, managers share the events and new ideas that emerged on that group's most recent trip. Another organization, National Semiconductor, has "sharing rallies" where workers release their best knowledge to the rest of the company.

■ STEP 13: Acquire and Apply Technology

Learning organizations need to acquire and apply the best technology to help capture learning and release knowledge. Organizations that lack such information technology or that can't adequately use the technology they have are at a severe disadvantage. If learning is the journey, then technology is the road. Without it, you will not go anywhere very quickly.

Specifically, technology affects the quantity and quality of organizational learning. It speeds the flow of information, stores more information than non-electronic methods, is easier to update, provides better access to more people, and helps make organizational learning more exciting for workers.

One particular electronic system-electronic performance support systems (EPSS) is becoming more and more popular in organizations that want to focus on learning. An EPSS lets workers learn when and where they best can. It is especially useful as an on-the-job training tool. Because an EPSS responds to employees with explanations, definitions, descriptions, demonstrations, practice activities, assessments, feedback, and other resources as needed, the employees can learn while remaining productive.

For more information on EPSS, see *Info-line* No. 9806, "EPSS and Your Organization."

■ STEP 14: Encourage, Expect, and Enhance

A learning organization promotes learning at three levels—the individual worker, the group or team, and the organization itself. All three levels complement and invigorate each other, so none of them should be neglected when it comes to learning. Following are some ways an organization can encourage, expect, and enhance learning at each level.

Make learning a part of the job. Rover, for example, clearly states that everyone in the organization has two jobs: his or her current job, and learning how to do that job better.

Promote responsibility. Managers should expect each department and person to take responsibility for their own learning. Organizations can provide continuous learning packages that encourage workers to view learning as an everyday experience and to use every available opportunity for learning.

Encourage team learning. Team learning is the ability of a group to think and learn together. Ways to develop team learning include providing new job assignments, having workers participate in team projects, developing in-house activities geared toward teams (such as quality training), and asking groups to assess the organization's learning efforts.

Make learning organization-wide. Plan and implement learning activities on an organization-wide basis. This is the level at which systems thinking and learning are most possible. Also, turning knowledge into action is easier at this level because the links between learning, resources, and organizational power are clearer.

■ *STEP 15: Learn*
Understandably, to help your organization focus on learning, you need to know more about learning organizations.

Read. The literature on learning organizations grows every day. The American Society for Training and Development's Learning Organization Forum has a bibliography of over 350 articles and books in the field.

Attend conferences. This is a good way to learn theory as well as network with practitioners in the learning organization field.

Use in-house activities. Invite a leader of a learning organization to speak. Or have a leading consultant or researcher in organizational learning theory and practice present his or her ideas. Arrange for in-house workshops and discussions on the topic of learning organizations with a panel of subject matter experts.

Network. Identify successful learning organizations in your industry both in your geographic region and around the world. Talk to people in the organizations and listen to their ideas. Benchmark their organizations for learning skills and systems. You can keep the networking ball rolling by creating or joining a consortium of companies that want to become learning organizations.

Ernst and Young, one of the "Big Six" accounting firms, has undertaken all these options as part of its efforts to build a learning organization. Recently, the firm held a two-day seminar titled "Valuing the Learning Organization: A Symposium to Establish the Concepts, Language, and Metrics for Measuring Human Capital in the Knowledge Era." Panelists and participants included many of the top business and academic leaders in the learning organization field who discussed common issues and created action plans for their respective organizations. Other companies holding such conferences include TRW, Arthur Andersen, and Rover.

■ *STEP 16: Adapt and Improve*
The one idea that is clear to all companies on the road to becoming learning organizations is that a successful organization is never completely there. Perfection is unattainable, so learning can never end. Organizations must continually uncover, analyze, and adapt new knowledge and best practices. Those that stop learning risk failure, as did many of the "excellent" companies identified in Thomas J. Peters and Robert H. Waterman's *In Search of Excellence.* These companies began to lose profits and customer satisfaction. In some cases, the companies were bought out by the competition. Their flaw? They had stopped learning.

References & Resources

Articles

Argyris, C. "Double Loop Learning in Organizations." *Harvard Business Review,* September-October 1987, pp. 11-25.

Calvert, G., S. Mobley, and L. Marshall. "Grasping the Learning Organization." *Training & Development,* June 1994, pp. 39-43.

Galagan, P. "The Learning Organization Made Plain." *Training & Development,* October 1991, pp. 37-44.

Garvin, D. "Building a Learning Organization." *Harvard Business Review,* July-August 1993, pp. 78-91.

Jaccaci, A. "The Social Architecture of a Learning Organization." *Training & Development,* November 1989, pp. 49-51.

Kim, D. "The Link Between Individual and Organizational Learning." *Sloan Management Review,* Fall 1993, pp. 37-50.

Marquardt, M. "Systematic Links." *Best Practices,* September 1995, pp. 29-33.

———. "Building a Global Learning Organization." *Industry and Higher Education,* August 1995, pp. 217-226.

Marsick, V., et al. "Action-Reflection Learning." *Training & Development,* August 1992, pp. 63-66.

Nonaka, I. "The Knowledge-Creating Company." *Harvard Business Review,* November-December 1991, pp. 96-104.

Schein, E. "On Dialogue, Culture, and Organizational Learning." *Organizational Dynamics,* Autumn 1993, pp. 40-51.

Taylor, S. "Managing a Learning Environment." *Personnel Management,* October 1992, pp. 54-57.

Audiotapes

Crum, T, and J. Warner. "Discovery: A Model for Continuous Learning." ASTD No. 93AST-M66, from the 1993 ASTD International Conference.

Gibb, P. "Creating the Learning Organization." ASTD No. 93AST-Th6, from the 1993 ASTD International Conference.

Books

Chawla, S., and J. Renesch (Eds.) *Learning Organizations: Developing Cultures for Tomorrow's Workplace.* Portland, OR: Productivity Press, 1995.

Dixon, N. *The Organizational Learning Cycle.* New York: McGraw-Hill, 1994.

Marquardt, Michael. *Building the Learning Organization.* New York: McGraw-Hill, 1996.

———, and A. Reynolds. *The Global Learning Organization.* Burr Ridge, IL: Irwin, 1994.

Owen, H. *Riding the Tiger: Doing Business in a Transforming World.* Potomac, MD: Abbott, 1991.

Pedler, M., J. Burgoyne, and T. Boydell. *The Learning Company.* London: McGraw-Hill, 1991.

Peters, Tom., and R.H. Waterman, Jr. *In Search of Excellence.* New York: Harper & Row, 1982.

Peters, Tom. *Thriving on Chaos.* New York: Knopf, 1987.

Redding, J. *Strategic Readiness: The Making of the Learning Organization.* San Francisco: Jossey-Bass, 1994.

Senge, Peter., et al. *The Fifth Discipline Handbook: Strategies and Tools for Building a Learning Organization.* New York: Doubleday, 1994.

Senge, Peter. *The Fifth Discipline.* New York: Doubleday, 1990.

Vogt, J.F., and K.L. Murrell. *Empowerment in Organizations.* San Diego, CA: University Associates, 1990.

Watkins, K., and V. Marsick (Eds.) *In Action: Creating a Learning Organization.* Alexandria, VA: American Society for Training and Development, 1996.

———. *Sculpting the Learning Organization.* San Francisco, CA: Jossey-Bass, 1993.

Info-lines

Beil, D. "Fundamentals of Quality." No. 9111.

Chang, R.Y. "Continuous Process Improvement." No. 9210.

Raybould, B. "EPSS and Your Organization." No. 9806.

Simmerman, S. "Basics of Employee Empowerment." No. 9105.

Younger, S.M. "Learning Organizations: The Trainer's Role." No. 9306.

Zulauf, Carol. "Systems Thinking." No. 9703.

Steps to Becoming a Learning Organization

1. Commit to becoming a learning organization.

2. Connect learning with business operations.

3. Assess the organization's capability on all five learning organization systems: people, technology, knowledge, learning, and the organization itself.

4. Communicate the vision of a learning organization.

5. Recognize the importance of systems thinking and action.

6. Demonstrate and model a commitment to learning.

7. Transform the organizational culture to one of continuous learning and improvement.

8. Establish corporate-wide strategies for learning.

9. Cut bureaucracy and streamline the structure.

10. Empower and enable employees.

11. Extend organizational learning to entire business chain.

12. Capture learning and release knowledge.

13. Acquire and apply the best of technology to the best of learning.

14. Encourage, expect, and enhance learning at the individual, group, and organizational levels.

15. Learn more about learning organizations.

16. Continuously adapt, improve, and learn.

Job Aid

Learning Organization Profile

Below is a list of statements. Read each one carefully, then decide the extent to which it actually applies to your organization, using the scale below.

4 = applies fully
3 = applies to a great extent
2 = applies to a moderate extent
1 = applies to little or no extent

Learning Dynamics: Individual, Group or Team, and Organization

1. We are encouraged and expected to manage our own learning and development. _____

2. People avoid distorting information and blocking communication channels, using such skills as active listening and effective feedback. _____

3. Individuals are trained and coached in learning how to learn. _____

4. Teams and individuals use the action learning process. (That is, they learn from careful reflection on problems or situations, and then apply their new knowledge to future actions.) _____

5. People are able to think and act with a comprehensive, systems approach. _____

Organization Transformation: Vision, Culture, Strategy, and Structure

1. Top-level managers support the vision of a learning organization. _____

2. There is a climate that supports and recognizes the importance of learning. _____

3. We learn from failures as well as successes. _____

4. Learning opportunities are incorporated into operations and programs. _____

5. The organization is streamlined—with few management levels—to maximize communication and learning across all levels. _____

People Empowerment: Employee, Manager, Customer, and Community

1. We strive to develop an empowered workforce able to learn and perform. _____

2. Authority is decentralized and delegated. _____

3. Managers take on the roles of coaching, mentoring, and facilitating learning. _____

4. We actively share information with our customers to obtain their ideas to learn and improve services and products. _____

5. We participate in joint learning events with suppliers, community groups, professional associations, and academic institutions. _____

Job Aid

Knowledge Management: Acquisition, Creation, Storage and Retrieval, and Transfer and Use

1. People monitor trends outside our organization by looking at what others do—for example, by benchmarking best practices, attending conferences, and examining published research. _____

2. People are trained in the skills of creative thinking and experimentation. _____

3. We often create demonstration projects to test new ways of developing a product or delivering a service. _____

4. Systems and structures exist to ensure that important knowledge is coded, stored, and made available to those who need and can use it. _____

5. We continue to develop new strategies and mechanisms for sharing learning throughout the organization. _____

Technology Application: Information Systems, Technology-Based Learning, and EPSS

1. Effective and efficient computer-based information systems help our organizational learning. _____

2. People have ready access to the information superhighway—for example, through local area networks, the Internet, ASTD Online, and so on. _____

3. Learning facilities such as training and conference rooms incorporate electronic multimedia support. _____

4. We support just-in-time learning with a system that integrates high-technology learning systems, coaching, and actual work into a single, seamless process. _____

5. Electronic performance support systems enable us to learn and to do our work better. _____

Grand Total for Five Subsystems (Maximum Score: 100)

81–100 Congratulations! You are well on your way to becoming a learning organization.

61–80 Keep on moving! Your organization has a solid learning foundation.

40–60 A good beginning! Your organization has gathered some important building blocks to become a learning organization.

Below 40 Watch out! Time to make drastic changes if you want to survive in a rapidly changing world.

Knowledge Management

Issue 9903

Knowledge Management

AUTHOR:

Amy Newman
Organization Blueprint, Inc.
195 Mayfair Avenue
Floral Park, NY 11001
Tel.: 516.328.8129
E-mail: anewman@
    orgblueprint.com
Web: www.orgblueprint.com

Amy Newman is co-principal of
Organization Blueprint, Inc.,
which helps companies increase
intellectual capital through organizational and employee development. She has worked as a training
and HR internal consultant. Amy
holds an M.S. degree in Human
Resource Management.

Editor
Cat Sharpe

Associate Editor
Sabrina E. Hicks

Production Design
Anne Morgan

ASTD Internal Consultant
Phil Anderson

Knowledge Management

If you want to know how to turn data and information into reusable knowledge, you want to know about "knowledge management." At its most basic definition, managing knowledge means finding ways to create, identify, capture, and distribute organizational knowledge to the people who need it.

The Knowledge Imperative

Why is knowledge management such an important issue for organizations today? Several factors contribute to this "knowledge imperative."

■ *Competitive Advantage*
Factors such as increasing competition, globalization, and the new knowledge economy make sustained business growth more difficult than ever. Decreasing product differentiation, more market players, and reduced time to market make it tough to compete. Clearly, we have moved into an era where many companies view knowledge as their most competitive advantage.

■ *Technology*
Technology has influenced our rate of change and requires an adaptable, skilled, and educated workforce. Work is increasingly complex—partly because of technological changes and the race for market share and revenue. But technology has also given us wonderful opportunities to share information as never before; it is an enabler of learning and has helped training professionals rethink how people learn inside and outside the classroom.

■ *Organizational Changes*
Who has not experienced organizational changes beyond his or her imagination in the past decade? Downsizing, mergers and acquisitions, initial public offerings (IPOs), restructuring, and the like have all influenced the way organizations operate. Unfortunately, in our haste to achieve the "lean and mean" mantra of the 1980s, we have stripped our organizations of some of their valued history and social norms—those tangibles that organizations rely on to do business.

By downsizing some of the more experienced, older workers, companies have released critical knowledge of what has worked—and what has not worked—in the past. When a company forgets important learnings from years past, we call this "corporate amnesia." We can also think of this as a "Ground Hog Day" phenomenon: Every six months or so, we tend to repeat the same mistakes over and over again.

■ *Employment Flexibility*
Knowledge is also more transient than ever before, with employees making career and job changes more often and more employees opting to be "free agents" by taking contract or consulting work. In addition, companies that rely on outsourcing are in danger of losing critical knowledge within their own organization and becoming too dependent on outside firms.

This business environment has led us to look at knowledge management opportunities with great optimism.

Definitions

What do we mean by "knowledge"? The consulting company Ernst & Young, one of the leaders in managing internal knowledge, may have the best definition of all: "What people need to know to do their jobs." Plain and simple.

Our job in managing knowledge is to figure out how to turn information into reusable, useful knowledge and create, identify, capture, and distribute knowledge to the people who need it. Part of the trick is using what is in everyone's heads (that is, tacit knowledge that is not easily expressible, such as experience and values) and making it more explicit (that is, describing this knowledge in a formal and systematic manner, often by expressing it in words and numbers).

Have you ever said to yourself, "I wish we knew what we know"? Are you hoping to identify, and ultimately benefit from, what the organization knows? Then you are hoping for knowledge management.

Continuum: Data to Knowledge

Place knowledge on a continuum, with data at one end and knowledge at the other. "Data" are unorganized words, numbers, or images (for example, a stock quote). As we move along the continuum, "information" is data processed into meaningful patterns, for example, a stock trend. "Knowledge" is information that is put into productive use and is actionable. Knowledge is most valuable to an organization because it can be reused once shared.

Data	Information	Knowledge
unorganized numbers, words, or images	data processed into meaningful patterns	information put into productive use and made actionable

This *Info-line* will help you understand why knowledge management is important for your organization. After defining knowledge management, this issue poses questions to help you identify the intellectual capital you need to manage. It also introduces the new roles, opportunities, and technology you can expect when you begin to manage knowledge. Finally, with the job aid to guide you, this issue will help you determine if your organization is ready for knowledge management.

Intellectual Capital

We need to begin by deciding what knowledge is most important to your organization. Thomas A. Stewart defines "intellectual capital" in his book by the same name: "Intellectual capital is intellectual material—knowledge, information, intellectual property, experience—that can be put to use to create wealth. It is collective brainpower."

The following are examples of intellectual capital:

- information about customers

- effective practices (for example, audit practices or system processes)

- market and technology trends

- patents

- trademarks

- information about employees

- innovations

- information about competitors

- competencies

- industry knowledge

- decisions and decision-making processes

Stewart warns us, "We all spout goop about the importance of the human asset; the fact is, some employees are indeed immensely valuable assets but others are merely costs, and grumpy ones at that." Our job is deciphering which knowledge—and which people—are most critical to organizations.

Take a minute to think about your own organization:

- What examples of intellectual capital or key knowledge exist in your organization (the business needs)?

- Think about your training curriculum and key priorities for the coming year. There should be a connection between the focus of your training efforts and how you answered the first question.

- What are the barriers to this knowledge getting transferred throughout the organization?

Typically, people in organizations do not share knowledge; some organizational cultures do not support sharing. The following barriers are common:

- You are not rewarded for sharing.

- The appearance that you are wasting time if you are "just thinking" or if you are talking to someone casually.

- The timing is not right for sharing—unless you need the information right now, it is meaningless to you.

- It takes too long to figure out where to get information; you do not know where to start.

- It seems like a waste to cull through 99 percent of useless data for 1 percent meaningful knowledge.

- You are just too busy—it is not worth the time.

- If you ask for help, it looks like you cannot do your job.

- You do not want to share information or knowledge because you believe that you will not be as valuable to the organization.

You cannot conquer any of these barriers overnight. Overcoming them is part of the process of creating a culture of knowledge sharing and is part of the puzzle of knowledge management.

Puzzle Pieces

In many ways, knowledge management is built on the concepts of the "learning organization." Approaching knowledge management strategically, we can apply systems thinking—which we have learned from Peter Senge's popular work *The Fifth Discipline*. The ideal way to build organizational knowledge is to use a holistic, integrated approach.

To answer the critical question, "What is our organization's most important knowledge and what is the best way to share it?", you conduct the same type of needs analysis needed to strategically determine training priorities. Consider both *business* and *people* issues, which include intellectual capital. (Refer to the *Organizational Analysis for Knowledge Management* sidebar on the following page.)

Based on the puzzle pieces presented in the sidebar, think about your answers to the following:

- What are your organization's strengths for supporting knowledge management (for example, good employee rewards system or strong leadership)?

- What are your organization's constraints for improved knowledge management (for example, unclear business strategy or distrustful culture)?

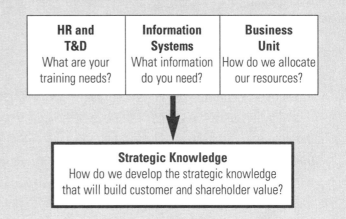

A New Way of Thinking

This illustration, developed by Probe Consulting, presents how the separate departments of Human Resources (HR) and Training & Development (T&D), Information Systems, and the Business Unit each sees its contribution to the organization. With the new way of thinking, however, each of these groups would merge and share the goal of developing strategic knowledge, which builds customer and shareholder value.

HR and T&D	Information Systems	Business Unit
What are your training needs?	What information do you need?	How do we allocate our resources?

Strategic Knowledge
How do we develop the strategic knowledge that will build customer and shareholder value?

For a more detailed list of questions, refer to the *Organizational Analysis for Knowledge Management* sidebar. If you are interested in reading more on systems thinking or learning organizations, refer to *Info-lines* No. 9703, "Systems Thinking" and No. 9602, "16 Steps to Becoming a Learning Organization."

New Roles and Opportunities

Traditionally, trainers asked questions about training. Now we know that is not enough. With a more strategic view of learning, we need to rethink our paradigms. In the sidebar above, Probe Consulting, a leading knowledge management consulting firm, describes an interesting perspective on "old thinking" and an emerging new way of thinking.

The idea of different departments merging and sharing the goal of developing strategic knowledge is new to most organizations; therefore, several companies have created chief knowledge officer (CKO) or chief learning officer (CLO) positions to oversee learning and knowledge management. Typically, a CKO is responsible for knowledge management, while a CLO may have responsibility for

Organizational Analysis for Knowledge Management

You need to consider both the *business* and *people* issues when deciding what knowledge is most important to your organization and how you should share that knowledge. Think through the following questions, based on the puzzle pieces for business and people issues demonstrated below. They are best asked during interviews with executives and focus groups of employees. Linking these issues together is important for a solid foundation in determining the best approach to knowledge management for your organization.

Business Analysis

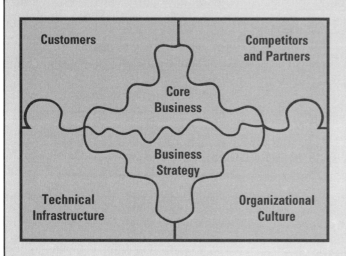

People Issues

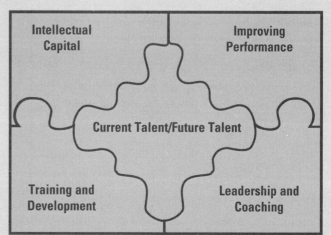

■ Business Strategy

1. My company's strategy over the next one to three years is to _____ .

2. Our successes include _____ .

3. Our failures include_____ .

4. We are frustrated about _____ .

■ Core Business

1. We are able to keep up to date with technology, products, customers, and competitors by _____ .

2. Innovations and new ideas are introduced by _____ .

3. We built on our core business by _____ .

■ Customers

1. My company's customers are _____ .

2. Our customers can best be described as _____ .

3. My company demonstrates its focus on customers by _____ .

4. We measure customer satisfaction by _____ .

■ Competitors and Partners

1. My company works closely with these other firms: _____ .

2. Our competitors' business is different from ours in these ways: _____ .

3. We partner with other firms to _____ .

■ *Organizational Culture*

1. Our company is organized in this way: _____ .

2. We are organized this way because _____ .

3. Decisions are made by _____ .

4. Our organizational culture can best be described as _____ .

■ *Technical Infrastructure*

1. The systems we have in place include _____ .

2. These systems help our business to _____ .

3. Other systems we need are _____ .

People Analysis

■ *Current Talent*

1. The most important competencies include _____ .

2. Our high performers are rewarded by _____ .

3. We value teamwork and demonstrate its importance by _____ .

4. Our turnover statistics indicate _____ .

5. We have a career development program in place to _____ .

6. If our executives needed to be replaced, we would be prepared by _____ .

■ *Future Talent*

1. When we have a staff opening, we _____ .

2. We recruit by _____ .

3. We select new staff based on _____ .

4. a new employee starts at our organization, we _____ .

■ *Intellectual Capital*

1. My company's intellectual capital includes _____ .

2. We know who our knowledge assets are by _____ .

3. Knowledge is shared in these ways: _____ .

4. The systems we use to manage knowledge include _____ .

■ *Training and Development*

1. The key skills people need to learn are _____ .

2. Training is offered to _____ .

3. Our staff knows what training is available by _____ .

4. We measure the results of learning by _____ .

■ *Improving Performance*

1. My company measures individual performance by _____ .

2. Staff goals are communicated by _____ .

3. Feedback is given to staff by _____ .

4. Our performance management system includes _____ .

5. When someone is not performing, his or her boss _____ .

■ *Leadership and Coaching*

1. In my organization, leaders are chosen because _____ .

2. The leaders in my organization all have these skills: _____ .

3. Leaders are trained in these ways: _____ .

4. We can tell that our leaders/managers operate as a team because _____ .

organizational learning. The following responsibilities are the three most important responsibilities of these positions:

1. Build a knowledge culture.

2. Create a knowledge management infrastructure.

3. Show an economic payoff.

It is critical that the person in the role of CKO or CLO builds bridges between training, human resources, information systems, and the business units. Too often, knowledge management efforts focus on the technology and miss the bigger picture of organizational learning.

Positioning a CKO or CLO is just one of the ways many training departments have begun the transition from traditional training to more comprehensive learning solutions. Business-focused training departments are transitioning from trainers to performance consultants and already trainers possess many of the skills and experience that are required to embrace knowledge management, such as the following:

- has knowledge of adult learning theory

- uses different media for training, such as computer-based training (CBT), Web-based training (WBT), self-study, videos, audiotapes, and classroom training

- acts as facilitator and communicator

- translates raw data to knowledge

- groups knowledge into learnable segments

This expertise positions trainers perfectly to lead knowledge management initiatives. Many trainers lack a strong knowledge of technology and of how it enables the learning process. Working with information systems helps trainers see the possibilities, and helps technologists understand the value, of strategically planned learning and competency development. Because of the benefits of working with information systems, some companies are combining all or part of their training departments with the information systems department to create true performance-focused organizations.

But CKO and CLO positions are not the only opportunities for trainers. Trainers could take on new roles, such as the following:

- facilitating or administering a knowledge database or network

- managing learning resources (including knowledge management systems)

- acting as an information or knowledge broker

While using technology is often an effective way to manage knowledge, we need to expand learning activities to include other ways for people to learn from each other, which include the following:

- team learning
- action learning
- coaching and mentoring

Info-lines on the topics above are available and included in the *References & Resources* section of this issue.

Ways to Manage Knowledge

Technology is an enabler; thus, there are some wonderful examples of using technology to help people manage knowledge.

First, review the following solutions that use technology (or "techknowledgy"). For all of these solutions, it is essential for you to work with other departments in the organization. Depending on

12 Ways to Measure Intellectual Capital

The Montague Institute, an education affiliate of Limited Edition Publishing (a knowledge base publishing company), cited the following 12 techniques that you can use to place value on intangible assets.

1. **Relative value.** Bob Buckman of Buckman Laboratories and Leif Edvinsson of Skandia Insurance are proponents of this approach, in which the ultimate goal is progress, not a quantitative target. Example: Have 80 percent of employees involved with customer in a meaningful way.

2. **Balanced scorecard.** Supplements traditional financial measures with these additional perspectives: customers, internal business processes, and learning or growth. The term was coined by several Harvard Business School professors.

3. **Competency models.** By observing and classifying the behaviors of successful employees and calculating the market value of their output, it is possible to assign a dollar value to the intellectual capital they create and use in their work.

4. **Subsystem performance.** It can be relatively easy to quantify success or progress in a particular aspect of intellectual capital. For example, Dow Chemical was able to measure an increase in licensing revenues from better control of its patent assets.

5. **Benchmarking.** Involves identifying companies that are recognized leaders in leveraging their intellectual assets, determining how well they score on relevant criteria, and comparing your own company's performance against their performance. Example of a relevant criterion: Leaders systematically identify knowledge gaps and use well-defined processes to close them.

6. **Business worth.** This approach centers on these questions: What would happen if the information we now use disappeared? What would happen if we doubled the amount of key information available? How does the value of that information change after a day, a week, or a year? Evaluation focuses on the cost of missed or underutilized business opportunities.

7. **Business process auditing.** Measures how information enhances the value of a given business process, such as accounting, production, or marketing.

8. **Knowledge bank** Treats capital spending as an expense instead of an asset and treats a portion of salaries (normally 100 percent expense) as an asset because it creates cash flow.

9. **Brand-equity valuation.** Measures the economic impact of a brand (or other intangible asset) on such factors as pricing power, distribution reach, and ability to launch new products as line extensions.

10. **Calculated intangible value.** Compares a company's return on assets (ROA) with a published average ROA for the industry.

11. **Microlending.** A new type of lending that replaces tangible assets with such intangible collateral as peer-group support and training. Used primarily to spur economic development in poor areas.

12. **Colorized reporting.** Suggested by SEC commissioner Steven Wallman, this approach supplements traditional financial statements (which give a "black and white" picture) with additional information that adds "color." Examples: brand values and customer satisfaction.

©1997, The Montague Institute
www.montague.com

Case Study: Help Desk

In the early days of knowledge management (about 1994), an international company wanted to provide assistance to customer service representatives in each of its regional offices. The key objective was to lower costs by reducing customer site visits. Secondary objectives included the following:

- share knowledge to ensure that service representatives handled customer situations consistently

- cross-train representatives most effectively

- bring new hirers up to speed quickly

They designed and implemented a case-based reasoning (CBR) system, which consisted of scenarios describing product or technical problems and possible solutions. As a sophisticated model using a form of artificial intelligence, this was a tremendous effort.

There is good news from the original initiative:

- Help desk staff throughout the regional offices learned that sharing knowledge is critical to meet improved customer service and financial business goals.

- When Internet technology became available, the organization was primed to take advantage.

- The customer, product, and technology knowledge is still transferred and used throughout the organization.

- Some mechanisms for measuring the usefulness of knowledge have been preserved.

Today, at least one regional office has its own systems, some more refined and robust than others, each built in separate programs with separate rules and types of knowledge shared. They are sharing information, but are struggling a bit to find the best solution, even among product lines within their own location.

The global project manager summarizes the moral of the story: "The sirens of technology are out there. You cannot help being drawn to them, so play your hand skillfully (it's an expensive business, this knowledge management thing), and don't forget where you came from—you have an organization to run, it consists of people with egos and knowledge and customers/users, all awash in connectivity. Knowing what knowledge is most important and useful, and how it is used, and keeping the balance right among all this is very important."

the knowledge management system you select, you may need help—from inside or outside the organization—to classify, codify, and organize knowledge to create a "knowledge base." Also remember that too many knowledge management systems become "haunted houses"—which people never visit. All of the puzzle pieces described earlier need to be in place to support a good knowledge management system.

Solutions Using Technology

If you decide you want to use technology to help you and your employees share information, a variety of solutions are available. Below you will find some of the more popular technical solutions.

■ *Knowledge Management Architecture*
Lotus Notes™ is probably the most classic, pre-Web example of a database used for knowledge management. Several companies have been using databases of various sorts to manage knowledge for the past couple of years. Booz-Allen's Knowledge On-line (KOL) system has been operating since 1995. Consultants can log in and get access to "Experts/Resumes/History" and get information by colleague or topic. This design saves time recreating each other's work. Monsanto, a life science company, boasts a database that allows account managers to share information about customers and competitors.

Using a database, however, does entail some special requirements:

- keeping the database updated
- getting valuable information in
- making sure people are getting value out

The companies that do this most successfully have at least one person dedicated to managing the database.

■ *Electronic Corporate "Yellow Pages"*
Yellow Pages are becoming more common as a way for employees to find knowledge or knowledgeable people within an organization. Employees look up

experts by topic and can call on them for assistance. This is quite an effective way to help people learn from others' experience—as long as "experts" are truly subject matter experts and the culture of knowledge management is in place.

■ *Expert Network*

Similar to the Yellow Pages, this database includes external resources. Some databases include experts around the world who have specialized knowledge that does not exist within the organization.

■ *"Lessons Learned" Database*

Would you like for your employees to share how they applied something they learned in a training class? A lessons learned database helps people learn from others' successes and mistakes.

■ *Case-Based Reasoning*

This system has been most successful in customer service organizations, where complex problems can be solved using this system. The knowledge input into the system is in the form of cases, and users get answers to questions through a series of drill-downs until the precise case is determined.

■ *Embed Knowledge into Processes*

As we have learned with performance support systems, one of the most effective ways to help people learn and improve performance is to build learning into their job functions. Ernst & Young does this effectively in several processes, where consultants get work samples from other consultants just when they need them, during, for example, an audit.

■ *Intranet*

Many companies already have lots of knowledge, or at least information waiting to be transformed into knowledge. Organizing information on an intranet allows employees to find what they need for their jobs and acts as an effective tool for managing organizational knowledge.

Case Study: Management University

Managers of a software development group have attended a series of training programs designed to improve their management skills. Based on improvements in how managers dealt with staff and participant feedback surveys from the workshops, the programs were quite successful.

Senior management asked Organization Blueprint, Inc. for a recommendation to reinforce skills learned during the workshops and to continue the development of these managers. Because the managers are dispersed throughout the United States and the United Kingdom, consultants from Organization Blueprint worked with this organization to develop an intranet site, which they called "Management University," for all managers who attended the workshops. Management University is a virtual place where managers can build on current knowledge and learn from the experience and ideas of other managers. The site includes the following sections:

- a toolkit of searchable ideas, cases, and tips (such as motivating and retaining)

- a virtual library of resources and reference materials for managers (such as videos, books, articles, Web sites, and outside training programs)

- a message board/discussion area for managers to react to posted cases and to share ideas and ask for opinions on their own situations

- an option to "ask an expert" or a specific person for answers to tough questions or situations

- interviews and communications from executives, including what they have learned during their management career

- a calendar of upcoming workshops relevant to managers

Management University is an example of knowledge management at work. It is a place where managers can share learnings and experience with each other and continue their development—outside the classroom.

Knowledge Management Principles

Thomas H. Davenport and Laurance Prusak discuss the following principles of knowledge management in their book published by Harvard Business School, *Working Knowledge: How Organizations Manage What They Know*:

- Knowledge originates and resides in people's minds.

- Knowledge sharing requires trust.

- Technology enables new knowledge behaviors.

- Knowledge sharing must be encouraged and rewarded.

- Management support and resources are essential.

- Knowledge initiatives should begin with a pilot program.

- Quantitative and qualitative measurements are needed to evaluate the initiative.

- Knowledge is creative and should be encouraged to develop in unexpected ways.

Solutions Without Technology

Sometimes you do not have to use technology to manage knowledge. Described below are ways to manage knowledge without the assistance of technology.

■ *Talk Rooms*

One of the easiest solutions—again, as long as there is a culture of learning—is to establish a place for people with common concerns or interests to talk to each other. Because of the workplace issues we discussed earlier (such as being too busy to share information or fearing to share because you do not want to lessen your value to the organization), we often miss the easiest way to share knowledge: Take time away from our usual fire-fighting, and talk to each other.

■ *Communities of Practice*

Similarly, groups of employees can organize and share information around a practice, system, customer group, or process. Preferably, employees will do this on their own with only encouragement from management.

■ *Benchmarking and Best Practices*

While we no longer consider benchmarking and best practices new concepts, we should not forget about or underestimate the value of researching how other companies or areas of the company have implemented practices successfully. And because imitation is the best form of flattery, you should feel no shame in using what someone else learned and looking to others to prevent mistakes and rework.

■ *"Practice Olympics"*

The consulting firm of McKinsey & Company held off-site meetings, encouraging employees to share information and learnings. With Practice Olympics, you can organize employees into teams to compete for best ideas and practices. These activities help employees apply what has worked—and avoid what has not worked—in other areas of the organization. This is an excellent idea for team meetings and conferences to focus on continuous improvement.

Warning

A word of caution about all of the knowledge management possibilities: Information wants to be free. In some respects, "knowledge management" is an oxymoron because knowledge is messy and cannot really be held on to. Managing knowledge too tightly will kill it. The best approach is to provide resources and encouragement to people, without managing how sharing takes place (see the *Knowledge Management Principles* sidebar at left).

How to Get Started

The new world of knowledge management is a challenge for most of us. (See *Competencies to Manage Knowledge* sidebar on the following page for the new competencies it will take to be successful.) The planning worksheet, which follows the competencies sidebar, is designed to prepare you for a knowledge management briefing for your organization.

Knowledge management is not a fad. The Gartner-Group, a high-tech consulting firm and leading authority on information technology, makes the following strategic planning assumption: "Knowledge management is currently a hot concept, but expect a period of disillusionment over the next three to five years, followed by widespread adoption."

Training professionals can prevent disillusionment in the organization, by working with other departments to make strategic knowledge management pay off. To ease the transition, remember to do the following:

- Think through barriers and how to work around them.

- Prepare the organization to care about knowledge management.

- Help managers value and manage knowledge (see *Briefing Worksheet* on page 96).

- Help employees learn to learn.

- Focus on high-value knowledge.

- Keep knowledge management in the context of broader organizational learning.

- Find someone who will champion your first initiative: Use a pilot group.

- Help groups identify knowledge-sharing methods that will work for them.

- Identify, develop, and take care of the people who hold the knowledge.

Training professionals and training departments have enormous opportunities to lead the knowledge management effort at a more strategic level, for the good of the entire organization. Many knowledge management efforts fail, often because technology drives the effort without the assistance of people who know most—and probably care most—about how real learning takes place.

With the above tips in mind, you will be on your way to transforming the training department—and training professionals—to lead the charge towards organizational learning and knowledge management.

Competencies to Manage Knowledge

To be successful with knowledge management, your entire organization must be up for the challenge. The lists below describe characteristics that your staff must adopt if knowledge management is to succeed.

All Staff

- Is open to self-learning.
- Demonstrates reflection.
- Takes appropriate risks.
- Learns by mistakes.
- Generates new knowledge.
- Accesses knowledge from many sources—internal and external.
- Embeds knowledge in processes, products, and services.
- Transfers existing knowledge around the organization.
- Uses accessible knowledge in decision making and problem solving.

All Managers

- Maintain a long-term perspective.
- Promote personal and professional learning.
- Invest in training activities for staff.
- Value knowledge and encourages communities of interest.
- Maintain knowledge management systems.
- Facilitate knowledge growth through culture and incentives.
- Measure the value of knowledge assets and knowledge management.
- Use intellectual capital for competitive advantage.
- Apply technological innovation for competitive advantage.

Training Staff

- Aligns training with business strategy and goals.
- Analyzes training needs from a business perspective.
- Chooses appropriate training methodology, including videos, CD-ROMs, computer-based training (CBT), Web-based training (WBT), classroom training, learning groups, reference materials and databases, videoconferencing, and so forth.
- Keeps current with and applies new learning/training developments.
- Develops and uses measurement criteria and can assess effectiveness of initiatives.
- Participates actively in cross-functional groups as a business partner.
- Has a network of internal and external training/development resources and consultants.
- Knows the financial implications of training decisions.
- Understands and uses technology in developing learning solutions.

Training and HR Leaders

- Act as a change agent within the organization.
- Participate in the annual organization planning process.
- Are called-on as an internal consultant by all levels of management.
- Are organization-savvy.
- Demonstrate leadership skills within the organization and within external professional organizations.
- Are results-oriented.
- Can mobilize commitment to a new initiative.
- Seek integrated solutions to business needs.

Planning Worksheet

Use this worksheet to prepare for a briefing on knowledge management within your organization. Check each item off after you have answered it completely and honestly.

Current Knowledge Management Systems

Given your assessment of the most critical knowledge your organization needs to develop or share, answer the following questions.

☐ In what areas of your organization is knowledge being systematically shared? (Consider knowledge—for example, competency data—in your own department that may be used more effectively by others.)

_____

_____

☐ How does this system work?

_____

_____

☐ Can other areas use it?

_____

_____

☐ In what areas of your organization is knowledge shared informally?

_____

_____

☐ Does this work?

_____

_____

☐ Does this knowledge need to be shared across the organization?

_____

_____

Training Department

☐ Who else in the training or HR department will assist you in spearheading a plan to manage knowledge more effectively?

_____

_____

☐ How can they help foster information sharing with their clients in other areas of your organization?

_____

_____

☐ How will you manage this new project with the existing work of the training department?

_____

_____

Next Steps

☐ What barriers exist in your organization? How can they be overcome?

Barriers	Solutions
1. _____	1. _____
2. _____	2. _____
3. _____	3. _____
4. _____	4. _____
5. _____	5. _____
6. _____	6. _____
7. _____	7. _____
8. _____	8. _____

☐ How will you prepare employees and managers to care about sharing knowledge?

_____

☐ Which executives would be likely to champion knowledge management in your organization?

_____

☐ What do you need to do to get them to do this?

_____

_____

Briefing Worksheet

This worksheet provides the sketch of an itinerary for a knowledge management briefing. Use it to help you prepare a knowledge management briefing for your organization.

Introduction

● Session goals.

_____
_____
_____
_____
_____
_____

● Why knowledge management is important to us.

_____
_____
_____
_____
_____
_____

● Business context.

_____
_____
_____
_____
_____

Intellectual Capital

● Definition.

_____
_____
_____
_____
_____
_____

● What is our intellectual capital?

_____
_____
_____
_____
_____
_____

● How are we managing our intellectual capital?

_____
_____
_____
_____
_____
_____

● Brainstorming: what else can we do?

_____
_____
_____
_____
_____
_____

Action Planning

● Next steps.

_____
_____
_____
_____
_____
_____
_____
_____
_____
_____
_____
_____
_____
_____
_____

References & Resources

Articles

Allee, Verna. "12 Principles of Knowledge Management." *Training & Development,* November 1997, pp. 71-74.

Bassi, Laurie. "Harnessing the Power of Intellectual Capital." *Training & Development,* December 1997, pp. 25-30.

Bassi, Laurie, et al. "Trends in Workplace Learning: Supply and Demand in Interesting Times." *Training & Development,* November 1998, pp. 51-75.

Clark, Ruth Colvin. "Recycling Knowledge with Learning Objects." *Training & Development,* October 1998, pp. 60-63.

Cohen, Sacha. "Knowledge Management's Killer App." *Training & Development,* January 1998, pp. 50-57.

Davenport, Thomas, et al. "Successful Knowledge Management Projects." *Sloan Management Review,* Winter 1998, pp. 43-57.

Galagan, Patricia A. "Smart Companies." *Training & Development,* December 1997, pp. 20-24.

Greengard, Samuel. "Storing, Shaping and Sharing Collective Wisdom." *Workforce,* October 1998, pp. 82-88.

Johnson, Paul. "Managing Knowledge Assets Over the Web." *CBT Solutions,* May/June 1998, pp. 1+.

Martinez, Michelle Neely. "The Collective Power of Employee Knowledge." *HRMagazine,* February 1998, pp. 88-94.

Mayo, Andrew. "Memory Bankers." *People Management,* January 22, 1998, pp. 34-38.

Parks, Eric R., and Scott Russell. "Web-based Knowledge Acquisition Gets SMART." *Technical Training,* January/February 1998, p. 36.

Pascarella, Perry. "Harnessing Knowledge." *Management Review,* October 1997, pp. 37-40.

Rowland, Hilary, and Lynn Harris. "Doctor Know." *People Management,* March 5, 1998, pp. 50-52.

Stevens, Larry. "Linking Together." *Human Resource Executive,* March 5, 1998, pp. 46-49.

Stewart, Thomas A. "Is This Job Really Necessary?" *Fortune,* January 12, 1998, pp. 154-155.

Stuller, Jay. "Chief of Corporate Smarts." *Training,* April 1998, pp. 28-34.

Van Buren, Mark E. "Virtual Coffee Klatch." *Technical Training,* September/October 1998, pp. 42-46.

Watkins, Karen E., and Mary Wilson Callahan. "Return on Knowledge Assets: Rethinking Investments in Educational Technology." *Educational Technology,* July/August 1998, pp. 33-40.

Books

Brooking, Annie. *Intellect Capital; Core Assets.* International Thomson Publishing, 1998.

Davenport, Thomas H., and Laurance Prusak. *Working Knowledge: How Organizations Manage What They Know.* Boston: Harvard Business School, 1998.

De Geus, Arie. *The Living Company.* Boston: Harvard Business School, 1997.

Friedman, George. (ed.) *The Intelligence Edge: How to Profit in the Information Age.* Crown Publishing, 1997.

Nonaka, Ikujiro, et al. *The Knowledge-Creating Company: How Japanese Companies Create the Dynamics of Innovation.* Oxford University Press, 1995.

Schank, Roger C. *Virtual Learning: A Revolutionary Approach to Building a Highly Skilled Workforce.* McGraw-Hill, 1997.

Senge, Peter. T*he Fifth Discipline: The Art & Practice of the Learning Organization.* New York: Doubleday/Currency, 1990.

Stewart, Thomas A. *Intellectual Capital: The New Wealth of Organizations.* New York: Doubleday, 1997.

Tobin, Daniel R. *The Knowledge-Enabled Organization.* New York: AMACOM, 1998.

Info-lines

Raybould, Barry. "EPSS and Your Organization." No. 9806.

Darraugh, Barbara. "Coaching and Feedback." No. 9006.

Marquardt, Michael. "16 Steps to a Learning Organization." No. 9602.

———. "Action Learning." No. 9704.

Zulauf, Carol Ann. "Systems Thinking." No. 9703.

Internet Sites

KNOWLEDGE On-line
www.knowledge.org.uk

Knowledge Management at APQC
www.apqc.org

Ready for Knowledge Management?

Need an aid to help you determine if your organization is ready to manage knowledge strategically? Answer the following questions by circling the number (1, 2, or 3) that corresponds with your answer of *definitely not, somewhat,* or *definitely.* After you have recorded an answer for each question, calculate your score by adding up the numbers you circled. Compare your score with the chart located below the questionnaire to find out if your organization is ready for knowledge management.

	Circle One		
	Definitely Not	Somewhat	Definitely
1. My company's strategy for the next one to three years is clear. I understand the goals and priorities that are most critical to the organization.	1	2	3
2. The most critical knowledge that my organization needs to acquire or share has been defined and is well known throughout the organization. We know what *intellectual capital* is our competitive advantage.	1	2	3
3. How we recruit and retain people is closely linked to our business strategy, customer needs, and organizational knowledge needs.	1	2	3
4. The people who are most important to your business have been identified and are sufficiently valued and taken care of.	1	2	3
5. We have a communications strategy in place that fits into our corporate culture, including various media (for example, management briefings, e-mails, brochures, newsletters, intranet, and so forth).	1	2	3
6. Our organizational culture supports learning and sharing of information and ideas. People are rewarded for taking risks and encouraged to learn from making mistakes.	1	2	3
7. Human resources and training initiatives will support the rollout of a knowledge management system. Programs include the following: • competency identification • learning activities • career development • succession planning • behavioral based interviewing • performance management system	1	2	3
8. My training organization successfully completes the following: • gets the right training to the right people when they need it • uses various media to deliver training (such as intranet, videos, documentation, classroom, CD-ROM, and so forth)	1	2	3
9. We have benchmarked with other companies and know which knowledge management solutions are best for the organization.	1	2	3
10. The leaders in my organization support staff development and believe in investing for future learning development.	1	2	3

Scoring

☐ **25-30 *Ready!*** You and your organization are well positioned for a successful knowledge management initiative.

☐ **20-24 *Close.*** You and your organization are on your way, but you need to take a closer look at some organizational issues to ensure a successful implementation.

☐ **10-19 *Stop!*** You are not yet at the stage of organizational readiness. Review the ideas presented in this issue, find some champions in your organization, and start promoting knowledge management.

Systems Thinking

Issue 9703

AUTHOR:

Dr. Carol Ann Zulauf
Zulauf & Associates
20 Briggs Street
Quincy, MA 02170
Tel. 617.573.8089
E-mail: czulauf@acad.suffolk.edu

Dr. Carol Zulauf designs and delivers training programs for various clients in the areas of systems thinking, organization learning, leadership development, and self-managed teams. In addition to her consulting practice with clients such as Motorola, Inc., Dr. Zulauf is also an Assistant Professor of Adult and Organization Learning at Suffolk University in Boston.

Editor
Cat Sharpe

Associate Editor
Patrick McHugh

Designer
Steven M. Blackwood

Copy Editor
Leanne Eline

ASTD Internal Consultant
Dr. Walter Gray

Reprinted 1998

Systems Thinking

The Process of Systems Thinking

"Organizational learning is a set of processes and structures for supporting continuous learning in the workplace. It is a process for facilitating people's ability to create new knowledge, share the understanding, and continuously improve themselves and the results of the organization."

—Diane Weston

Imagine for a moment this rather common scenario happening in your organization:

The members of the sales staff go to an off-site meeting to determine how to increase sales. One of the options they decide to implement is to bundle training into the sale of your company's new product line. The problem with this option is that the training department was not represented in making that decision. The added demands come as a surprise to the training people and they are not prepared for it. Trainers are getting burned out from the increasing requests for their services. This dynamic begins to decrease the common resource of the organization: training. Now if systems thinking had been applied to this particular situation—if the sales staff had evaluated the impact of their decision on other parts of the organization—other, much more effective results would have ensued.

Every organization strives for continuous improvement. Systems thinking affords you one opportunity for accomplishing this task. To begin, let's first position systems thinking as one of the key disciplines of organizational learning. In fact, it has often been referred to as the cornerstone discipline. According to author Peter Senge, organizational learning is a process within organizations in which people at all levels, individually and collectively, are continually increasing their capacity to learn and to produce results they really care about. For more information on organizational learning, refer to *Info-line* No. 9602, "16 Steps to Becoming a Learning Organization."

Systems thinking lets you look at a problem from a holistic perspective. It puts a problem into a context of the larger whole with the objective of finding the most effective place to make an appropriate intervention. With systems thinking you can try to determine what underlying, fundamental relationships are causing the problem, rather than being in a situation where you are forced to react and continuously "put out fires." And how many of us can easily relate to that predicament?

Systems thinking can also help you identify and respond to a series of changes before those changes lead to disaster. In systems circles, it will help you to avoid becoming like a boiled frog. For those of you who are unfamiliar with the boiled frog story, here it is:

If you take a live frog and put it in a pan of hot water, the frog will jump right out. But if the frog is placed in a pan of cool water that is gradually heated up, the frog will happily remain in the water and allow itself to be cooked to death.

This story relates to those organizational systems that are set up to react only to changes larger than a quantifiable amount and so, cannot respond to changes falling below a specified threshold. As long as the change is slow enough, it will not trigger a response until it's too late. Systems thinking allows you to recognize and work with any series of small changes, adapting and making plans that will benefit you and your organization—before the situation reaches a crisis stage.

Benefits of Systems Thinking

Employing systems thinking means you will be able to better understand the ramifications of your decisions. You will be able to assess a situation and determine where to make the most effective intervention. The following benefits have been attributed to using systems thinking:

- more knowledge, the right questions are asked
- stakeholders are involved in the process
- all acquire a shared understanding of the problem
- many perspectives are considered and integrated
- visions are beyond day-to-day events
- key decision makers take a long-term view
- see the big picture as a competitive advantage

For some specific examples of how organizations use systems thinking to their advantage, see the case studies on page 107 and page 109. The results of these cases illustrate how systems thinking has significantly improved processes and work environments.

Characteristics of Systems Thinking

When you start to think systemically, you will notice that the way you look at any and all problems will begin to change. Of course, these changes will take time and are part of a gradual process, but they do encompass a transformation in your thinking process. This change will have long-lasting and beneficial effects, both professionally and personally. As a systems thinker, you will be able to:

- Understand complex relationships and interdependencies.

- Take responsibility to fix the problem.

- Balance the short-term and long-term needs and perspectives.

- Reframe an issue or problem.

- See the entirety of a situation.

- Discern the patterns of recurring problems not driven by daily events.

- Question any and all underlying assumptions.

- Develop understanding and compassion.

Applying Systems Thinking

It is at this point where we can begin to apply the basic principles of systems thinking. These principles are based on Draper L. Kauffman's book *Systems 1: An Introduction to Systems Thinking* and Peter Senge's text *The Fifth Discipline Fieldbook*.

■ *No Final nor Right answers*
When you are dealing with a complex system and its many interdependencies, the main objective is to look for the best place to make an intervention—the place that will have the highest leverage in helping to solve the problem.

■ *Cause/Effect Indirectly Related to Time/Space*
When looking for the highest leverage to solve the problem, you will first need to look back over time to find the root cause. The leverage to solve the problem will not always be found near the symptoms of the problem.

■ *Solutions Require Thoughtful Consideration*
There will be time delays with any solutions you propose. These delays need to be considered when making a decision. For example: Your staff is becoming burned out because they have been working a lot of overtime hours. You decide to bring in a consultant to deliver training to your staff on how to manage this stress. The amount of time it takes to acquire the training and then implement the stress reduction strategies is a factor to consider when putting together a plan.

■ *Behavior Gets Worse Before It Gets Better*
As we go through the process of modifying a system, there will be some resistance to change. Behavior may go from bad to worse during this process. As members of the group begin to see the benefits of the shift in thinking, new patterns of behavior begin to emerge.

■ *Be Aware of Inherent Limits in Every System*
Nothing can grow forever. Eventually limits will be reached and an awareness of these limits to growth is an essential first step in learning how to manage a system.

■ *Foresight Benefits You in the Long Run*

Solutions to problems affecting complex systems usually take some time to resolve. If you wait until a problem suddenly develops and then are forced to react to the situation, you probably won't have enough time to determine the best possible solution. If, on the other hand, resources are allocated toward a plan that anticipates potential problems, you will have more choices open to make the kind of decision that is valuable to your organization.

The next section provides some examples of ways to detect and evaluate a problem from three different perspectives.

Perspectives of Systems Thinking

You notice that three trainers just quit last Friday. What would you do in this situation? We all have the tendency to react to events similar to this one—panic. However, if we step back for a moment and try to see the bigger picture that may be causing this particular situation, we will get a much better understanding of the hows and whys of the situation. First, take a look at the diagram below depicting the three ways or perspectives from which we can view a problem.

The situation described illustrates the "events" level, that is, *something* happened and the first response is to simply react to that *something*.

The next level, "patterns," takes us a step deeper into the problem. By having determined how many times something has happened, the process of seeing a pattern develop begins. To refer back to the trainer situation discussed earlier, a meeting with human resource personnel indicates that in addition to the trainers who quit, other employees also gave their notice to leave: five sales people, four engineers, and seven customer service representatives. This departure trend created a pattern that differs from the normal pattern.

Viewing a problem from the "structures" level, enables questions to be asked. Specifically, "What underlying structures are producing the patterns of behavior that we are seeing with this problem?" In other words, what is or are the underlying root cause(s) for why employees are leaving the organization. In this particular scenario, when the training manager began inquiring why people were leaving, it became evident that a key organizational decision

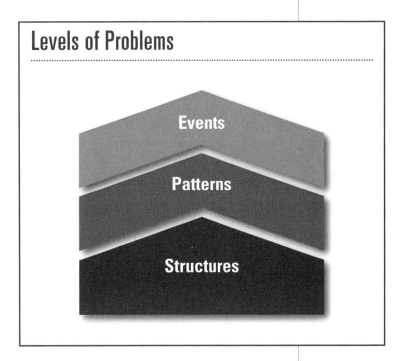

Levels of Problems

made several weeks earlier was responsible for the mass exodus.

In response to the company's low financial returns for the previous six months, top management decided to cease publication of a weekly performance update for employees. This decision stopped the information flow and fed into the employees' fears that the company was failing. The employees' subsequent move was to seek employment elsewhere.

This example points to a key element of systems thinking: When you decide to take an action, you need to ask what ramifications that action will have in an organization, both above and below the level at which the decision was made. Management policies and decisions can create confusion and can unwittingly be the source of a faltering system. By dealing with the elements at the level of the underlying structure, you will be increasing your leverage toward finding workable solutions to the organization's problems.

Implementing Systems Thinking

Whether you are just learning systems thinking or you are in a position to train others on the subject, you will find endless opportunities to learn and apply the principles of systems thinking in all aspects of your work and personal life. Over the next several pages, the steps to learning how to think systemically will be described. You will also have the opportunity to read actual case studies in the training area and decide where the most effective intervention should be made.

Step 1: Stating the Problem

Issues and problems are all around us, all the time. We normally don't have to look too far to find them and sometimes they even find us! Think about a problem or issue that you are dealing with and state it as clearly and succinctly as you can. This is the first step in learning to think systemically. Here are some examples:

- An employee consistently late to work.

- One-third of the sales force cannot effectively close a deal.

- Low course evaluations for one particular instructor drop even further.

- The training manager is into turf-building.

- Too many people expend too much energy "putting out fires."

- A marketing employee just turned away an ordering customer because "that is the salesperson's job."

Clearly stating a problem goes a long way to help you focus in on a potential solution. The next step is to expand on the problem as you have stated it. The best way to do this is to come up with the events or story behind the problem.

Step 2: Telling the Story

As an example for how to flush a story out, we will use one of the hypothetical problem statements listed above: "The training manager is into turf-building."

Two years ago, Michael had been hired as the manager of employee training and development for a 7,000-person telecommunications organization. In addition to the employee training and development manager, there are two other positions in the training department: a manager of sales training and a manager of technical training.

As one of their responsibilities, each manager had to submit a budget to the director of education; these budgets were based on the projected costs to operate their respective programs. Included in each budget was a line item designated for educational supplies and resources, but the dollar amount was allocated across the entire training department.

From the start, Michael worked to protect his turf. Regardless of what other training programs were offered by the other managers, he decided on the training programs he wanted for "his people," and publicly announced that he didn't "care what the other trainers were doing." He also wanted to make sure that he was the first person to secure common resources for his own programs—ordering books, journals, videotapes, and software.

Over time, Michael's behavior led to a duplication of programs, increased costs, and a decrease in the overall effectiveness of training as measured by the organization's 360-degree evaluations. In the process, Michael found himself becoming isolated from decisions, from his peers, and from social events.

When anyone tells a story, you begin to sense the following:

■ *Cause and Effect Flow to the Story*
The cause and effect results are readily apparent in the sample case. Michael is the first to put his requests in for supplies; there is now less money in the budget for others to use. Because Michael does not care that he is running a management development course in addition to the one being run by the Sales Training department, there is a duplication of effort.

■ *Certain Key Variables Emerge*

These key variables or tangible components reveal the impact of the story as it is unfolding. *For example, Michael's actions comprise one variable; the decrease in effectiveness of the training is another variable.*

■ *Affinity Amid the Components of the Problem*

This shows how a decision that is made affects other parts of the same department or the organization as a whole. *The actions taken and behavior displayed by Michael are detrimental to both the Training department and the whole organization.*

Step 3: Identifying Key Variables

Variables are those components in the story that change over time. There is also an inherent relationship between these variables. You will want to choose only those variables that are relevant to your story. Using the turf builder example from above, you can identify these other variables:

- manager's decisions and actions
- duplication of training programs offered
- costs
- effectiveness of training
- training department budget
- isolation

When these key variables from the turf builder scenario are put together, they tell the story of what transpired.

A couple of things to remember when selecting variables:

- They can have both quantitative and qualitative descriptors.

- Use nouns instead of verbs.

Moving From Events to Structure

Linda Booth Sweeney is a researcher at the Massachusetts Institute of Technology in the area of systems thinking and organizational learning. In her article, "Life-Long Systems Thinking," she has posed a sample of questions that can be asked in order to begin the process of moving from event-level thinking to structural-level thinking.

Sweeney says that to practice moving from events to structure, you can start by simply paying attention to the questions you ask. Try asking questions that get at deeper meanings, inquire into others' viewpoints, or elicit additional information. Following are some examples:

- Questions that look for patterns: *Has this same problem occurred in the past?*

- Genuinely inquisitive questions that enable information to be shared: *"What makes you say that?"*

- Questions that search for a deeper understanding of the problem: *"What structures might be causing this behavior?"*

- Questions that look for time delays: *"What effect will project delays have on our resources?"*

- Questions that inquire into unintended consequences: *"What would happen if we implemented this particular solution?"*

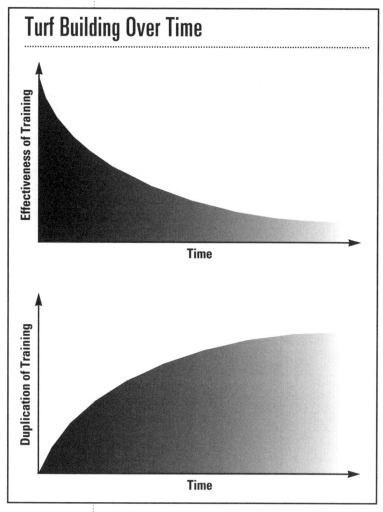

Turf Building Over Time

(graph 1 — vertical axis: Effectiveness of Training; horizontal axis: Time)

(graph 2 — vertical axis: Duplication of Training; horizontal axis: Time)

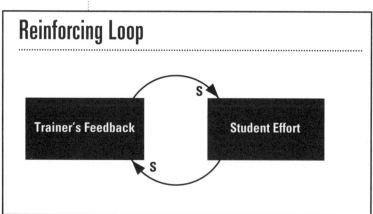

Reinforcing Loop

Trainer's Feedback → S → **Student Effort** → S →

Step 4: Visualizing the Problem

The old adage that a picture is worth a thousand words is exactly what this step produces. By taking the key variables identified above, we can create a visual graph of the existing problem. This, in a glance, will capture the pattern of the problem's behavior over time. Appropriately, it is referred to as a *behavior over time* graph. The benefit of drawing a *behavior over time* graph is that it allows you to quickly view the main dynamics of the problem and how it changes over time. If a variable increases, decreases, or remains the same, even after implementing an intervention, you will be able to detect the change.

The actual creation of a *behavior over time* graph is fairly simple. On the horizontal axis is time, and on the vertical axis is the key variable that you are concerned with. The graph shown at left has been produced to visualize the turf building example discussed above.

Step 5: Creating Loops

In this step, we take our story and draw it as a causal loop diagram. A causal loop diagram illustrates which factors influence other factors. When a story is illustrated in this manner, we can begin to understand the underlying dynamics of the situation, and equally important, determine the most effective point at which to make an intervention. There are two types of causal loops: reinforcing loops and balancing loops. Let's take a look at what each one means.

Reinforcing Loops

Reinforcing loops can be seen as akin to a self-fulfilling prophecy, in which one action, either positive or negative, influences another action.

For example, you have noticed a direct link between a trainer's positive feedback and the amount of effort expended by the student. In other words, the more positive feedback the trainer gives to the student, the more effort they put into the class. In a causal loop diagram, it would look like the diagram at left.

Reading the Loop. The loop indicates that as the trainer's positive feedback increases, the student's effort increases. As it happens in this case, the student's effort also increases and that feeds back to influence or increase the trainer's positive feedback. And the loop then becomes a self-perpetuating dynamic.

Take note of these special factors regarding reinforcing loops:

- Just as reinforcing loops can travel in a positive direction, they can also reverse into the negative direction. Try to read the loop again as if the trainer was withholding feedback or does not provide any at all.

- The arrowhead connecting the two variables— trainer's feedback and student effort—is called a "link."

- When you see an arrowhead with an *S* near it, this indicates that there is a change occurring in the same direction.

- When you see an arrowhead with an *O* near it, this indicates that there is a change occurring in the opposite direction. (See the figure on the next page and the explanation below.)

Balancing Loop

Balancing loops keep things in equilibrium. Much like the heating and air-conditioning system in your home that automatically regulates the temperature, a balancing system does exactly what it purports: balances.

Imagine you have just purchased a new computer-based training software package. Your instructional design team will need at least a month to learn and work with the new software before they can feel proficient in using it. We could say, in effect, that there is a gap between their current level of knowledge with this software and their desired level of knowledge and skill. In order to close this gap, adjustments (that is, training) will need to be conducted. The example illustrated on the next page represents a balancing loop.

Systems Thinking Applications at Ford

In the early 1990s, Ford Motor Company decided it wanted to move into systems thinking. The Executive Development Center in Dearborn, Michigan formed a group called the Systems Learning Network (SLN). This group was comprised of various individuals from differing parts of the company, each dedicated to learning systems thinking principles.

First, this group formulated a plan and then decided where to apply their new ideas. They began their thinking at the industry level and ultimately designed a computer simulation program that showed the interdependency of consumer demand and profitability.

Next, the group focused their efforts onto five on-site projects where they could apply the principles of systems thinking: electronics, electrical, manufacturing, product development, and central staff. With multiple initiatives running concurrently, the group could discover more about synthesizing the variables to create a whole picture. To achieve this goal, the SLN asked questions such as, "What could we understand about the whole that is greater than the sum of the individual projects?" "What do these applications tell us?" "How do we make progress from here?" Some of the key lessons acquired from the Systems Learning Network encompassed the following insights:

- Performance elements are interrelated.

- There is the need to start small and build complexity as you go. The real aim of systems thinking is to simplify complexity.

- It is important to energize and transform knowledge into programs, seminars, and projects in order to diffuse learning throughout Ford.

Vic Leo summed up the Systems Thinking initiative at Ford as follows: "The systems approach means to think in terms of interdependencies; to energize; to put forth a picture that represents a more desirable future, one that has a chance of dissolving the…mess…not recreating the…mess somewhere else or fixing it temporarily. And that was what the excitement at this manufacturing plant was all about."

Balancing Loop

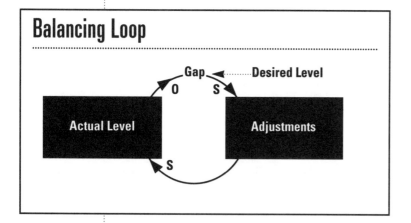

Reading the Loop. If there is a gap between the desired level and the actual level, adjustments or interventions—in this case, training—are made to close the gap. Begin at the point where the gap is located. As you go around the loop and adjustments increase, the actual level of attainment will also increase. When this occurs the gap *decreases*. Remember than an *O* link indicates a change in the opposite direction.

Additional considerations with loops are as follows:

- You can use both reinforcing and balancing loops to describe a problem. There is no rule stating that there can only be one type of loop.

- A balancing loop is fairly easy to recognize by adding the number of *O*s contained in the loop; an odd total sum is your indicator for a balancing loop.

Loops as Archetypes

Earlier it was stated that you could combine both reinforcing loops and balancing loops to describe a situation or problem. To accomplish this, you essentially take the loops and place them in a structure called an "archetype." An archetype is a generic configuration that can be applied to many different situations. It works much like a template.

One of the most common archetypes, "limits to growth" was introduced by Peter Senge in his 1990 book *The Fifth Discipline: The Art and Practice of the Learning Organization*. To define this archetype, most people have limits to growth structures. Essentially, this means that all individuals have a personal ceiling and to go beyond that limit requires an outside intervention.

The simplest way to recognize the limits to growth structure is through behavior patterns. Is there a situation in which things get better at first, and then mysteriously stop improving? First, you need to identify the reinforcing process—what is getting better and what is the action of activity leading to improvement? It might, for instance, be the story of an organizational improvement: an equal opportunity hiring program. The growing action is the equal opportunity program itself; and the condition is the percentage of women and minorities on staff. As the percentage of women in management increases, confidence in or commitment to the program grows, leading to a larger number of women in management. See the figure below.

Limits to Growth

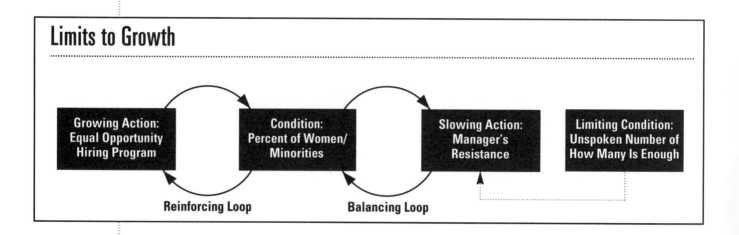

There is, however, bound to be a limiting factor. Typically, it is an implicit goal or a limiting resource. The second step is to identify the limiting factor. What slowing action or resisting force starts to come into play to keep the condition from continually improving? Some managers might have an idea in their minds of how many women or minority executives are "too much." That unspoken number is the limiting condition; as soon as that threshold is approached, the slowing action—manager's resistance—will kick in.

Now that we can delineate the problem through words, drawing an archetype that shows the interrelationships of the problem can visualize the situation. See the figure on page 46 as an example of an archetype that uses both reinforcing and balancing loops.

Other common system archetypes have been identified in Daniel Kim's book *Systems Thinking Tools: A User's Reference Guide*. These include a "drifting goals" archetype where there is a gap between the goal and the current reality. This gap can be resolved by taking corrective action or by lowering the goal. Corrective action takes more time, but will result in longer-term benefits; lowering the goal is more of a quick-fix solution.

Another archetype, called "shifting the burden," solves a problem by applying a symptomatic solution that diverts attention away from a more fundamental solution. For example: Management or human resources brings in an outside consultant who solves the problem for the organization, rather than acting as a catalyst in guiding the organization to take responsibility for and solve its own problems.

The last archetype is called "success to the successful," and can also be thought of as a self-fulfilling prophecy. If a person or group is given more resources than another person or group, the former has a higher likelihood of success than the latter. The initial signs of success also justify devoting additional resources to the former.

Case Study: STOL Group

The Systems Thinking/Organizational Learning (STOL) group at Milwaukee Area Technical College (MATC) has been laboring to understand their organizational dynamics. To accomplish this task, they have incorporated systems thinking as a core competency in their leadership effectiveness training as well as other core competencies of vision and reflective conversation.

Milwaukee Area Technical College is the largest two-year technical college in the United States. The college has more than 70,000 students, more than 3,000 employees, three unions, four campuses, and an annual operating budget exceeding $207 million. Founded in 1912, MATC underwent significant changes in the late 1980s and 1990s. In 1992, a new president had been hired for MATC and was charged with "cleaning up the mess" that had been left after the dismissal of the previous senior administrator.

At this point, the organizational culture of the institution was at a severely low ebb. Through the employment of systems thinking, the STOL group garnered an understanding of the dynamics at play in the college, and, by working with the president, was able to help develop systemic interventions that were sustainable over a specified time period. One of these was that the entire management team has been trained in systems thinking. The group's work has been instrumental in improving the institutional climate.

Effective Interventions

It is now time to take a step back and determine the most effective intervention. Let's use the *limits to growth* example.

If you were to suggest a solution to this problem, one that would have the potential for long-term change, what would it be? Most people try to solve *limits to growth* problems by pushing harder (in this example, by adding more programs, trying to convince senior management that the program is working, or just continuing to give it another chance). In the beginning, these strategies may be effective. However, the harder you push, the more the balancing process will resist your efforts. According to Senge, the point of leverage is in the balancing loop, not the reinforcing loop. Your task is to identify and change the limiting factor.

So, in our example, the task will be to work with the managers' resistance and to try to uncover the reasons behind their opposition. This usually requires a good deal of effort on your part; uncovering resistance involves engaging the manager in a dialogue that will uncover his or her deeply held thoughts, beliefs, and assumptions about management, control issues, and perceptions of power. Conducting these types of conversations actually encompasses one of the five disciplines of organizational learning, that of mental models.

Pulling It Together

We have come full circle in identifying the problem and the key place of intervention that promises the highest leverage in solving the problem. The hypothetical case study on the next page describes a scenario in which the skills of systems thinking can be applied. As an exercise, read the case study and then draw a behavior over time graph highlighting the key variables that have changed over time. Next, identify those variables that would tell a limits to growth story. Finally, decide where the key leverage point is—that point where you would make an intervention to help solve the problem.

Use the *Systems Thinking Template* found at left, as you work on the story. On pages 112–113, you will find an already completed template for the story, against which you can check your own work. You may find it beneficial to work on this case study with colleagues as you learn to practice your new skills in systems thinking.

Systems Thinking Template

Following is an outline of the steps you need to take in order to apply systems thinking to a given business scenario or problem.

		Completed	
Step 1:	Stating the problem	Yes	No
Step 2:	Telling the story	Yes	No
Step 3:	Identifying the key variables	Yes	No
Step 4:	Visualizing the problem	Yes	No
Step 5:	Creating the loops	Yes	No
Step 6:	Drawing the loops as an archetype	Yes	No
Step 7:	Determining the most effective intervention	Yes	No
Step 8:	Evaluating the whole process	Yes	No

Relevance to HRD and Training

There is a basic premise that human performance can be improved only when training is viewed and managed as a process within a system that transcends typical organizational and administrative boundaries. R. Brinkerhoff and S. Gill, in their book, *The Learning Alliance: Systems Thinking in Human Resource Development,* state that by understanding the principles of systems thinking and their impact on human resource development, we will begin to make this paradigm shift. According to F. Capra's and D. Steindl-Rast's text, *Belonging to the Universe: Explorations on the Frontiers of Science and Spirituality,* this shift is from breaking things down into different compartments or functional areas to interdependence; from seeing individual programs to viewing a process; from quick-fix to analytic solutions; and from short-term results to long-term results. Capra and Rast further state that the shift from parts thinking to whole thinking involves stepping back to see that the part is merely a pattern in an inseparable web of relationships.

One of the key steps in integrating systems thinking and training is to explicitly link training interventions and outcomes to business needs and strategic goals. This can be done by drawing a causal loop path between the training interventions and such outcomes as job behaviors and productivity. The path can show you where and in what ways the training results in measurable, high-leverage change.

Systems thinking encompasses looking at all the ramifications of your decisions and strategies. It asks you to question the types of behaviors you are rewarding. If you now reward the "fire-fighting" kind of reaction, what would happen in your organization if you started to reward people for making long-term, systemic changes? Systems thinking is not the latest management fad. It is a method of deep thinking that involves a shift in perspective to the whole of an organization, and in that process enables people to pause and reflect on what is really important. This way, actions that are undertaken are more imaginative, creative, and effective. Everyone comes out a winner with this kind of thinking.

A Hypothetical Case Study

A new senior manager has just been recruited into the Training and Education department. This department had been experiencing satisfactory results for several years and had an average yearly turnover rate of 5.6 percent.

Two months after joining the department, this senior manager informed everyone that the department was now going to be a self-managed team. He was quite enthusiastic about this change; and it spread to his staff. Some staff members were a little skeptical as to how to implement such a structure since the department was given *carte blanche* for proceeding with the implementation.

One particular employee took the initiative to organize training classes on what to expect from a self-managing team, what stages teams go through, what skills are needed, etc. This enabled the teams to get off to a good start. Staffers began communicating with one another and were ready to plan the implementation, organize the work flow, and determine how this change would impact their clients. Motivation was high; morale was heightened; productivity increased.

Word of the self-managed work team's efforts and subsequent success got around the organization. At this point, the new senior manager stepped in and told the self-managed work team members to hold off and to refer all future initiatives to his attention before starting anything. When any employee now offered up ideas, those ideas, as well as any requests for support and training, was stonewalled by the manager: The ideas were great, but could not be implemented now.

These delay tactics continued throughout the design and implementation phase of the self-managed work team structure. Meanwhile, the senior manager began his own programs, bringing in outside people to implement the self-managed team structure.

As for the team, their initial, pumped-up levels of morale, motivation, and productivity remained high for a period of time, but then began to decline. Turnover rose dramatically—up to 17 percent. Senior management was disappointed and upset by this downturn, but rallied behind the idea of self-managed work teams. "Stick together as a team, and the process will succeed," they told employees. The self-managed work team structure collapsed after 10 months.

Completed Business Story Template

Step 1: Stating the Problem

- A manager who has a tendency to thwart his staff's efforts.

Step 2: Telling the Story

- See the business story "Introducing Self-Managed Work Teams."

Step 3: Identifying Key Variables

- level of productivity, morale, and motivation

- turnover

- number of creative ideas from employees

- level of manager's support

- manager's basic need for control

- self-managed work teams

- number of roadblocks (bringing in own people, programs)

Step 4: Visualizing the Problem

- All of the above variables can be placed into a *behavior over time* graph to see how each one has changed over time (see Figure A at right).

Step 5: Creating the Loops

- Begin with the *manager's basic need for control*. Initially, this variable is rather low when the self-managed work teams are first introduced.

- As control is low, the manager's level of support is increased. (Remember that *Os* reflects a change in the opposite direction.)

- As support is heightened, the number of roadblocks is low. With no initial roadblocks, there is a growth in the number of creative ideas. Thus, the level of employee motivation, morale, and productivity also rises. (The *S* indicates a change in the same direction.)

- As motivation grows, the self-managed work team's level of success increases. The more successful the self-managed work team becomes, the more the manager's intrinsic need to control increases.

- With the need for more control, the manager's support to the team decreases. As the manager's support decreases, the number of roadblocks increase. This results in a reduction of creative ideas from employees. Eventually, the self-managed work team collapses.

*The point of emphasis in this particular scenario is that as the success of the self-managed work team increases, the manager's **need** for control increases (see Figure B at right).*

Step 6: Drawing Loops as an Archetype

- In a limits to growth archetype, the initial success of the self-managed work team creates better morale, increased productivity, self-sustaining motivation, and lower turnover.

- As these factors improve, slowing action tactics sneak into the picture, which then loop back to slow down the condition of morale, productivity, etc.

- The underlying reason is the limiting condition (that is, the manager's need for control).

(See Figure C at right.)

Step 7: Determining the Intervention Point

- The key leverage is to address the limiting condition, (that is, the manager's need for control).

Step 8: Evaluating the Whole Process

Questions to ponder:

- How did mapping the problem using systems thinking work?

- What worked well?

- How can this process apply to your own specific needs?

B= Balancing Loop   **R**= Reinforcing Loop

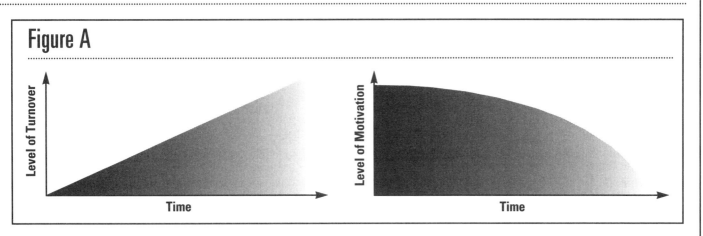

Figure A

Figure B

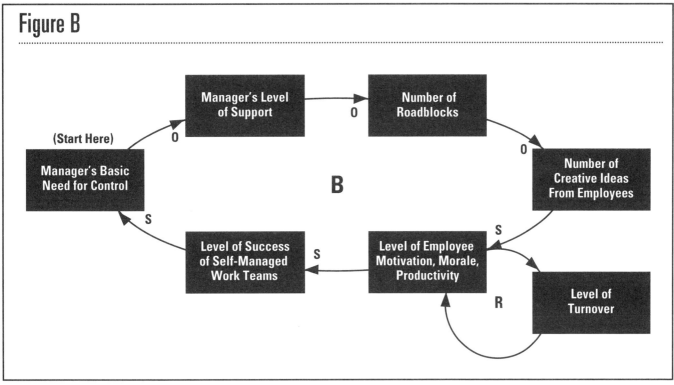

Figure C

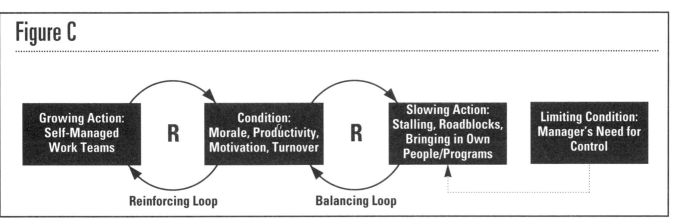

References & Resources

Articles

Argyris, C. "Good Communication that Blocks Learning." *Harvard Business Review,* vol. 72, no. 4, 1994, pp. 77-85.

Bernthal, P. "Evaluation That Goes the Distance." *Training and Development Yearbook,* 1996/1997.

Calvert, G. et al. "Grasping the Learning Organization." *Training & Development,* June 1994, pp. 39-43.

Corning, S. "Systems Thinking: Four Examples of Better Problem-Solving." *Healthcare Forum,* March/April 1990, pp. 22-24.

Filipczak, Bob. "Critical Mass: Putting Whole-Systems Thinking Into Practice." *Training,* September 1995, pp. 33-41.

Gallagan, Patricia. "The Learning Organization Made Plain: An Interview with Peter Senge." *Training & Development,* October 1991, pp. 37-41.

Garvin, D. "Building a Learning Organization." *Harvard Business Review,* July-August 1993, pp. 78-91.

Gephart, Martha A. et al. "Learning Organizations Come Alive." *Training & Development,* December 1996, pp. 34-45.

Huber, G.P. "Organizational Learning: The Contributing Processes and the Literature." *Organizational Science,* Vol 2, No. 1, 1991.

Issacs, William. "Dialogue: The Power of Collective Thinking." *The Systems Thinker,* April 1993.

Kim, Daniel. "From Event Thinking to Systems Thinking." *The Systems Thinker,* May 1996, pp. 6-7.

———. "Paradigm-Creating Loops: How Perceptions Shape Reality." *The Systems Thinker,* March 1993.

Kim, Daniel H., and Peter M. Senge. "Putting Systems Thinking into Practice." *System Dynamics Review,* vol. 10, no. 2-3, 1994.

The Language of Links and Loops." *The Systems Thinker,* October 1996, p. 12.

Marquardt, Michael. "Systematic Links." *Best Practices,* September 1995, pp. 29-33.

Schein, Edgar H. "How Can Organizations Learn Faster?" *Sloan Management Review,* Winter, 1993.

Senge, Peter M. "The Art of the Learning Organization: The Fifth Discipline." *Soundview Executive Book Summaries,* 1990, p. 5.

Senge, Peter M., and Colleen Lannon. "Managerial Microworlds." *Technology Review,* July 1990.

Stata, R. "Organizational Learning— The Key to Management Innovation." *Sloan Management Review,* Vol. 30, No. 3, 1989.

Stroh, Peter, and Wynne W. Miller. "Learning to Thrive on Paradox." *Training & Development,* September 1994, pp. 28-39.

Sweeney, L. "Life-Long Systems Thinking Practice." *The Systems Thinker,* October 1996, p. 6.

Thomas, J.B., et al. "Strategic Sensemaking and Organizational Performance: Linkages Among Scanning, Interpretation, Action, and Outcomes." *Academy of Management Journal.* vol. 36, no. 2, 1993.

Books

Argyris, C. *Knowledge For Action: A Guide to Overcoming Barriers to Organizational Change.* San Francisco: Jossey-Bass, 1993.

Anderson, Virginia, and Lauren Johnson. *Systems Thinking Basics.* Cambridge, Massachusetts: Pegasus Communications, 1997.

Beckhard, R., and Wendy Pritchard. *Changing the Essence: The Art of Creating and Leading Fundamental Change in Organizations.* San Francisco: Jossey-Bass, 1992.

Brinkerhoff, Robert O., and Stephen J. Gill. *The Learning Alliance: Systems Thinking in Human Resource Development.* San Francisco: Jossey-Bass, 1994.

Brookfield, Stephen D. *Developing Critical Thinkers: Challenging Adults to Explore Alternative Ways of Thinking and Acting.* San Francisco: Jossey-Bass, 1987.

Brooks, A., and K. Watkins (eds.). *The Emerging Power of Action Inquiry Technologies. New Directions for Adult and Continuing Education 63.* San Francisco: Jossey-Bass, 1994.

Capra, Fritjof, and Steindl-Rast, D. *Belonging to the Universe: Explorations on the Frontiers of Science and Spirituality.* San Francisco: Harper Collins, 1991.

Chawla, Sarita, and John Renesh. *Learning Organizations: Developing Cultures for Tomorrow's Workplace.* Portland, Oregon: Productivity Press, 1995.

Goodman, Michael, et al. *Designing a Systems Thinking Intervention: A Step-by-Step Process for Leveraging Change.* Cambridge, Massachusetts: Pegasus Communications, 1997.

Hodgson, A. "Hexagons for Systems Thinking." In Morecroft & Sterman (eds.) *Modeling for Learning Organizations*. Portland, Oregon: Productivity Press, 1992.

Johnson, Lauren. *From Mechanistic to Social Systemic Thinking: A Digest of a Talk by Russell L. Ackoff.* Cambridge, Massachusetts: Pegasus Communications, 1996.

Kauffman, Draper L., Jr. *Systems 1: An Introduction to Systems Thinking.* Minneapolis, Minnesota: Future Systems, Inc., 1980.

Kim, Daniel H. *Systems Archetypes I: Diagnosing Systemic Issues and Designing High-Leverage Interventions.* Cambridge, Massachusetts: Pegasus Communications, 1992.

———. *Systems Archetypes II: Using Systems Archetypes to Take Effective Action.* Cambridge, Massachusetts: Pegasus Communications, 1994.

———. *Systems Thinking Tools: A User's Reference Guide.* Cambridge, Massachusetts: Pegasus Communications, 1995.

Kim, Daniel H., and Colleen Lannon. *Applying Systems Archetypes.* Cambridge, Massachusetts: Pegasus Communications, 1996.

Mai, Robert P. *Learning Partnerships: How Leading American Companies Implement Organization Learning.* Alexandria, Virginia: American Society for Training & Development, 1996.

Marquardt, Michael. *Building the Learning Organization: A Systems Approach to Quantum Improvement and Global Success.* New York: McGraw-Hill, 1996.

Marquardt, Michael, and A. Reynolds. *The Global Learning Organization.* New York: Irwin Publishing, 1993.

Morecroft, John D.W., and John D. Sterman. *Modeling for Learning Organizations.* Portland, Oregon: Productivity Press, 1994.

Morris, L. "Learning Organizations: Settings for Developing Adults." in *Development in the Workplace.* Hillsdale, New Jersey: Lawrence Erlbuam Associates, 1993.

O'Reilly, Kellie Wardman. *Managing The Rapids: Stories From the Forefront of the Learning Organization.* Cambridge, Massachusetts: Pegasus Communications, 1995.

Revans, Reginald. *The Origins and Growth of Action Learning.* Bromley, England: Chartwell Bratt, 1982.

Robinson, J. "Managerial Sketches of the Steps of Modeling." in Randers, Jorgen (ed.) *Elements of the System Dynamics Method.* Portland, Oregon, Productivity Press, 1980.

Sanford, Carol. *Systems: A Hierarchy of Types.* Battle Ground, Washington: Spring Hill Publications, 1993.

Schein Edgar H. *Organizational Culture and Leadership.* San Francisco: Jossey-Bass, 1992.

Senge, Peter M. *The Fifth Discipline: The Art and Practice of the Learning Organization.* New York: Doubleday/Currency, 1990.

Senge, Peter M., et al. *The Fifth Discipline Fieldbook: Strategies and Tools for Building a Learning Organization.* New York: Doubleday/Currency, 1994.

Vogt, Eric E., and Nancy Gottlieb. *The Art and Architecture of Powerful Questions."* Cambridge, Massachusetts: MicroMentor, 1994.

Watkins, Karen E., and Victoria Marsick. *Sculpting the Learning Organization: Lessons in the Art and Science of Systemic Change.* San Francisco: Jossey-Bass, 1993.

Watkins, Karen E., and Victoria J. Marsick (eds.). *In Action: Creating The Learning Organization.* Alexandria, Virginia: American Society for Training & Development, 1996.

Wheatley, Margaret J., and Myron Kellner-Rogers. *A Simpler Way.* San Francisco: Berrett-Koehler, 1996.

Info-lines

Marquardt, Michael. "16 Steps to Becoming a Learning Organization." No. 9602.

Other Resources

Leo, V. *Systems Thinking Applications: A Call to Action, Designing the Future at Ford.* Center for Organizational Learning, Massachusetts Institute of Technology. Working paper 14.001, (1993).

Senge, Peter M. "Transforming the Practice of Management." Paper presented at the *Systems Thinking in Action Conference,* November 1991 and in *Human Resource Development Quarterly,* San Francisco: Jossey-Bass, 1993.

Sweeney, Linda Book, and Dennis Meadows. *The Systems Thinking Playbook.* The Turning Pointing Foundation, 1996.

Job Aid

Systems Thinking Checklist

Use the following checklist to help you and your organization practice and implement systems thinking.

☐ Choose a recurring problem or issue in your organization.

☐ Set-up a discussion meeting for everyone affected by or interested in this problem.

☐ Define the problem or issue in as few words as possible (no more than 2 sentences).

☐ Verbalize the problem as a story, explaining the issue as an element of a larger picture.

☐ Visualize the problem by creating behavior-over-time graphs.

☐ Draw causal loop diagrams to capture the existing dynamics.

☐ Determine which systems archetype depicts the structure of the problem.

☐ In conjunction with colleagues, study and discuss the systems thinking tools (the graphs, diagrams, and archetypes) that have been constructed from the problem.

☐ Make any changes to the diagrams so that the archetype reflects reality.

☐ Focus on what changes can be applied and where such an intervention will bring you the highest leverage.

☐ Evaluate possible consequences of your intervention. Imagine a scenario of what would happen if the intervention were implemented. Identify potential pitfalls or roadblocks.

☐ Close the big loop. Implement the solution.

☐ Evaluate the effectiveness of the intervention in solving the initial problem.

Action Learning

Issue 9704

Action Learning

AUTHOR:

Michael Marquardt
President, Global Learning
    Associates
1688 Moorings Drive
Reston, VA 22090
Tel. 703.437.2060
FAX: 703.437.3725

Michael Marquardt is professor of
HRD at George Washington University and President of Global
Learning Associates. He has
assisted corporations worldwide in
initiating and implementing action
learning programs. He is also the
author of more than 50 books and
articles.

Editor
Cat Sharpe

Associate Editor
Patrick McHugh

Designer
Steven M. Blackwood

Copy Editor
Kay Larson

ASTD Internal Consultant
Dr. Walter Gray

Reprinted 1999

Solutions in Real Time

Action learning has quietly become one of the most powerful problem-solving—as well as team and organizational development—tools to be used all over the world. Companies as diverse as Exxon, General Electric, TRW, Motorola, Arthur Andersen, General Motors, the U.S. Army, and British Airways use action learning to develop their global executives, identify strategic competitive advantages, reduce operating costs, create performance management systems, and as the foundation for evolving into learning organizations.

And yet action learning is not utilized in most organizations. Why? Primarily because most people are unfamiliar with the basic concepts and capabilities of action learning. Secondly, some managers are unwilling to trust and delegate their power or control to action learning teams. And finally, some companies are not willing to provide the time action learning groups may require to systematically and simultaneously solve current problems and learn how to handle future challenges.

This *Info-line* describes what action learning is, how and why it works, and what benefits accrue to organizations that employ it. Several examples of companies successfully using action learning are also presented.

What is Action Learning?

Action learning is a group effort that involves solving real problems, focusing on acquired learning and implementing systems-wide solutions. It provides well-tested methods of accelerating learning that enable people to master and handle difficult situations. It also has a powerful, multiplying impact. By using action learning, organizations can more effectively respond to change as people apply new knowledge and skills in their daily work, and as the solution is applied to other related functions or processes. Action learning is the brainchild of Reg Revans, President of the International Management Center in the United Kingdom (see the box on the next page), who began creating and implementing action learning programs more than 50 years ago.

Action learning is not only a powerful tool for solving real problems, but also provides group participants with the leadership skills and self-awareness required to help the organization develop and adapt to the changing environment.

Action learning can address a wide variety of problems—complex problems that touch on different parts of the entire organization, problems that are not amenable to expert solutions, problems on which decisions have not already been made, and problems that are organizational rather than technical in nature. Examples of such problems could include the following:

- reducing turnover in the workforce
- improving systems to reduce paperwork
- increasing sales by a predetermined amount
- resolving problems between departments
- increasing the use of computers in a company
- reorganizing a department
- closing of a production or line
- increasing productivity
- developing a new performance appraisal system

Benefits of Action Learning

The power and multiplying impact of action learning is demonstrated by its many direct and indirect benefits, including:

- solutions to complex organizational problems
- individual and team development
- management development
- the creation of learning organizations

Problem-Solving

Solving problems, as well as resolutions of different tasks and issues within an organization, is a key focus and one of the unique facets of action learning. The numerous case studies described in this *Info-line* attest to the success of action learning in solving organizational problems.

Reg Revans—The Father of Action Learning

Reg Revans is *the name* that dominates action learning. A physicist from Cambridge, England, Revans began his journey in the 1920s when he observed how scientists who worked at the Cavendish Laboratory were able to share their problems—how they questioned each other and how they received support from their colleagues. No one individual person was considered more important than any other and each had a contribution to offer, even if they were not "experts" in a particular field. By working in this manner, the scientists generated workable solutions to all their problems.

In 1945 Revans became the first Director of Education and Training for the newly formed National Coal Board (NCB). Immediately after his arrival, Revans pronounced to the NCB staff college: "We do not envisage the permanent employment of a staff of qualified tutors to deliver lectures and seminars."

This having been said, Revans set about changing how things were done at NCB. He organized managers into small groups of four or five members and met with them in the coal fields, usually close to their own pits. From the start, these managers worked together trying to solve coal field problems—they visited each others' pits and operated as consultants to one other. In those mines that participated in the prototype action learning programs, output increased 30 percent per person, while at the nonparticipating mines, productivity remained static.

In his role as Professor of Industrial Administration, Revans, in 1955, addressed a turnover problem at the Royal Infirmary of the University of Manchester. The infirmary could not retain trained staff, particularly nurses. By involving those individuals who were seen as part of the problem to try to solve the problem, Revans discovered that nurses were often discouraged from asking questions and were thus, unable to fully comprehend their roles vis-a-vis the other people at the hospital. Small groups, composed of doctors, nurses, and administrators, worked on nearly 40 disparate projects and accomplished some impressive results. In later years, Revans achieved similar successes in Belgium working with government officials, business leaders, and various academicians.

In the 1970s and 1980s, Revans carried the concept of action learning to Australia, Malaysia, Singapore, Nigeria, and Egypt. He then became President of the International Management Center in Buckingham in 1982 where the first MBA program based exclusively on action learning was begun. In 1996 the first Action Learning Conference, hosted by Revans, was held in London and attended by 100 delegates from around the world.

Action learning sets, or the group of people involved in an action learning project, examine difficult tasks or problems in the organization. Then they act to change them and return the results to the organization for review and learning. While undertaking action learning, individuals build skills and create significant change as they begin addressing organizational problems from new perspectives.

Through action learning sets, problems are solved in much more innovative, systematic ways than through any other method. Action learning programs have been instrumental in creating new products and services, saving million of dollars, reducing delivery time, and changing organizational culture.

Individual and Team Development

Research and experience have demonstrated that action taken on a problem changes both the problem and the people acting on it. There are several skills and attitudes developed by participation in the action learning process:

- self-understanding and self-awareness from the feedback of others in the groups

- development of critical reflection and reframing skills, which allow a person to examine "taken-for-granted" assumptions that prevent an individual from acting in new and more effective ways

- questioning and problem-solving skills

- learning how to be an effective member of a group by being supportive as well as challenging

- enhanced formal presentation and facilitation skills

- new knowledge about the organization's products, people, and processes

- facilitation, advising, and leadership skills

- effective communication skills, including giving and receiving feedback

Management Development

During his lecture-based courses, Reg Revans noticed that the students and managers were relatively passive and lacking in energy in the classroom. They came to life, however, when they discussed their own "back home" problems with one another. The message was loud and clear to Revans: Managers are people of action who learn from action. They will help each other in the right environment and will be prepared to share their experience and insights.

In the real world of work, most managers learn by doing a job. Learning is rarely identified beforehand, however, and managers seldom know how to tap these learning opportunities.

In action learning sets, managers submit their actions to the constructive scrutiny of persistent but supportive colleagues. Through this process of enforced self-revelation, managers realize why they say the things they say, do the things they do, and value the things they value. The managers also begin to transcend a self-image built on the assumption that their actions are entirely congruent with their espoused intentions.

Action learning develops three attributes critically needed by managers who want to be effective in today's workplace of rapid change.

■ *Openness*
Learning to be truly open to the wide range of perspectives essential to identifying trends and generating choices means managers must be willing to suspend their need for control. In order to process multiple levels of experience, managers must recognize their own values, backgrounds, and experiences. They must also recognize that their own backgrounds or experience can be a fatal flaw.

■ *Systems Thinking*
This includes the ability to connect issues, events and data points—the whole rather than its parts. Framing structural relationships that resemble dynamic networks rather than staid, patterned interactions or relationships predicated on one's position in the hierarchy is important. With systems thinking, the collective learning of an organization becomes the basis of future competitive advantage.

■ *Creativity*
Increase personal flexibility and willingness to take risks; the ability to be innovative while encouraging, and rewarding creativity around the manager.

Task Forces and Quality Circles

Action learning groups are different from task forces or quality circles because action learning groups are charged with learning from real-world problems, assumptions that are challenged, and actions that are confronted. In task forces, on the other hand, the major goal is addressing the problem; any learning that occurs is incidental. Unlike task forces, action learning groups often address problems outside of their expertise. Addressing unfamiliar problems results in fresh perspectives and provides teams the opportunity to learn new problem-solving approaches. The focus is on a real work-centered project and action is expected.

In addition to individual and team learning, task forces and quality circles tend to focus on specific problems and tasks rather than on identifying the organization-wide, environmental, or systematic elements that must also be changed if effective, lasting change is to take place.

Case Study: Whirlpool

At Whirlpool, line managers serve as set facilitators for action learning programs. Tom Helton, former Director of Corporate Learning, proudly notes, "We have close to 100 percent of our line mangers actually conducting the action training. The role of training and HR people has become largely one of training line managers to be action learning facilitators."

Action learning group successes at Whirlpool include:

● A cross-functional team developed Whirlpool's award-winning super-efficient refrigerator.

● An action learning set devised a just-in-time system to supply product kits and components.

● Several cross-functional groups in Europe refined complex manufacturing processes.

● A team leveraged knowledge from North America into a new dryer designed specifically for European customers.

The last item above provides a good example of how action learning enabled Whirlpool to better provide for its European customers. When the North American version of Whirlpool's dryer was introduced in Europe, it was a complete failure due to its different size, color, and customized options that had been generated for a primarily American buyer. As a result of an action learning set that met, asked questions, and sought outside expertise, a new European-type dryer, smaller in scale and customized for that market was developed. The lessons learned allowed Whirlpool to apply these changes to other American products that would be offered abroad in the future.

Implementing Action Learning

The action learning group (also called a set or team) is the core entity in action learning. The group is composed of four to eight individuals who examine an organizational problem that has no easily identifiable solution. Ideally, the group should be diverse, allowing it to maximize various perspectives and obtain fresh viewpoints.

Over the years, action learning programs have typically developed into the following six fundamental elements:

1. An action learning group or team (referred to as a "set").

2. A project, problem, or task.

3. Questioning and reflection process.

4. A commitment to action.

5. A commitment to learning.

6. A group facilitator ("set advisor").

Action Learning Groups

Depending on the action learning problem, groups can be made up of individuals from across functions or departments. In some situations, groups are comprised of individuals from other organizations or professions such as the company's suppliers or customers. While many problems (developing a performance appraisal system or marketing strategy, for example) benefit from external, fresh perspectives and expertise, certain problems are perhaps best handled only with people internal to the organization (for example, handling a morale issue or combining two departments).

Though you want a diverse group, members should be near the same level of perceived competence so they feel comfortable challenging one another. The group dynamics and the diversity of its participants are the keys to success of the action learning set. The group, sometimes referred to as "fellows in opportunity" or "comrades in adversity" should include people who care about the problem, who know something about the problem, and who have the power to carry out the recommendations of the group. While the action learning group may occasionally call on external experts and specialists when desired, these experts should not be thrust on the group.

The group plays many roles for the "client" (who may be the organization or the individual with the project/problem). Groups can be a support network, a resource for information and ideas, a problem-solving forum, or a sympathetic constructive challenger. To be effective the group members should possess the following attributes:

- dedication to solving the problem

- ability to listen, to question self and others

- willingness to be open and learn from group members

- value and respect for others

- dedication to taking action and achieving success

- awareness of their own and others' ability to learn and develop

Projects or Tasks

One of the fundamental beliefs of action learning is that we learn best when undertaking action, which we then reflect on and learn from. A project or task gives the group something to focus on that is real and important, something that is relevant and important to them. It creates a "hook" on which to test stored-up knowledge.

There are several criteria to determine if the project is appropriate for an action learning group:

■ Reality
The project chosen by or for the group must be a real organizational problem, task, or issue that needs to be addressed. It exists in a real-time frame, such as how to adapt to a new culture or decrease time between design and production. The problem should be of genuine significance to the company. This rules out projects or tasks that are pulled out of a hat to give trainees a "realistic" problem. Additionally, the organization should want a tangible result by a definite date so as to justify the investment of time and funds.

Case Study: National Semiconductor

When poor delivery performance from the South Portland, Maine, manufacturing plant of National Semiconductor resulted in an inability to provide quality service for AT&T, the plant's senior management decided to do something. They selected eight people from several areas throughout the company and created a customer request improvement team to deal with the delivery performance problem.

Team members were chosen from sales, marketing, engineering, manufacturing, and planning. There was also a representative from AT&T. The group met two to three times a month over a 90-day period. At the end of this time period, the team had proposed close to 40 ideas to solve the problem. These ideas resulted in four key action initiatives:

- analyzing in new ways the delivery misses
- increasing the frequency of lead-time updates
- creating critical device lists
- developing pre-alert reports.

Following the implementation of these initiatives, AT&T recognized National Semiconductor as a "world-class" supplier. Working in action learning teams is also seen as a key tool for having increased productivity and creativity at National Semiconductor.

■ Feasibility
The project must be feasible; that is, within the competence of the group. For example, a group with no financial or legal knowledge should not work on those issues.

■ Authority
The task or issue should be within the group's sphere of responsibility or the group should be given the authority to do something about the problem such as including their recommendations in future employee orientation programs.

■ Type of Problem
The project should be a problem and not a puzzle. A puzzle can be defined as a perplexing question to which an answer or solution already exists; you just have not yet found it. A problem, on the other hand, has no existing solution. For example, an exercise to discover the legal requirements for reporting information to government agencies or contracted customers would be a puzzle, while finding better ways to communicate important

Case Study: General Electric

General Electric (GE) has declared action learning as a vital strategy for transforming GE "into a global-thinking, fast-changing organization." Action learning teams are built around organizational problems that are real, relevant, and require decisions. Formats may vary, but typically, two teams of five to seven people from diverse businesses and functions within GE work together on the problem. The company has built into the action learning projects opportunities for feedback to the participants on strategies and issues regarding leadership and teamwork skills. The participants also reflect on the total learning experience.

Besides team building, action learning has supplied GE participants with a framework for dealing with multicultural and global issues. Global action learning teams usually focus on potential new markets for the company. In a recent two-week executive development course for global business leaders held in Heidelberg, Germany, the action set spent week one building team and leadership effectiveness. They also met with key European business leaders, opinion makers, and government officials from France, Germany, and Sweden.

During the second week, focus shifted to GE projects—plastic, lighting and electrical distribution, and control busi-

nesses. One action learning team looked at the lighting strategy for Europe, which reflected the sharp rise—from 2 to 18 percent in 18 months—in GE's share of the western European consumer lighting market, due primarily to the acquisition of Tungsram in Hungary and Thorn Lighting in the United Kingdom. The teams were encouraged to be creative and think of serious ways GE could change the market and excite retailers and customers alike by finding new ways to add value.

The participants traveled across Europe to conduct interviews, get firsthand experience of how local culture, language, currency, legislation, tax laws, and consumer preferences for national brands effected purchasing. Between interviews, the participants debriefed one other and prepared their final reports to present to GE's top management, including CEO Jack Welch.

James Noel, manager of Executive Education at GE, acknowledges action learning has been pivotal to GE's recent successes; it has made "participants active partners in the learning process. Because the team projects provide value to GE's businesses, it has an immediate return on investment. Action learning also provides a viable vehicle for dealing with issues of leadership and teamwork."

information to people inside and outside the organization would be a problem. Different people will come up with different ideas and suggestions as how to solve it. There may be any number of possible solutions that might be satisfactory.

■ *Learning Opportunities*

The project should provide learning opportunities for members. It should also have possible applications to other parts of the organization such as marketing strategies developed for one product that can be applied to other products, or group dynamics that can be applied to other groups within the organization.

Questioning and Reflection Process

By focusing on the right questions rather than the right answers, action learning focuses on what one doesn't know as well as what one does know. Action learning tackles problems by first asking questions that clarify the exact nature of the problem, then

reflecting and identifying possible solutions, and finally taking action.

Action learning employs the formula $L = P + Q + R$; where: **Learning is equal to Programmed Instruction** (that is, knowledge in current use, in books, in one's mind, in organization's memory, and so on), **plus Questioning** (fresh insights into what is not yet known), **plus Reflection** (recalling, thinking about, pulling apart, making sense, trying to understand).

For example, where L is discovering how to motivate employees during a downsizing **is equal to P** (book knowledge, experience, expert advice, and others' experiences) **plus Q** (why did we end up downsizing, how can we most effectively work with our employees, and what are my skills in communicating and motivating?) **plus R** (why did the group develop these particular solutions, were we so creative or not so creative, did we consider all alternatives, and how effectively did we work as a team?).

Action learning builds upon the experience and knowledge of a group (the group's **P**), such as new concepts and ideas about downsizing, as well as its fresh questioning and reflective insights that can result in valuable, new learning for the organization and for the group.

P (knowledge) is traditionally used in most problem-solving activities. It allows for incremental, narrowly focused changes, but rarely for quantum improvements. If one takes only presently existing knowledge about supervision (or marketing or productivity or training), but does not put it into the context of the day-to-day operations of the organization *and* one's self-awareness about how well one performs, one's growth and development (as well as the organization's) will be slow and built solely on external sources of knowledge.

Groups are generally unable to solve problems from a systems perspective. **Q** and **R**, however, are what make the real difference in the quality of problem solving and provide opportunities for individual, team and organizational growth. Questioning and reflecting generates creativity, removes people out of boxes, identifies connections, and develops systems perspectives. Typical problem solving or quality circles focus more on symptoms because they do not get to the heart, to the deep systems-based causes.

The major difference between asking questions in action learning and asking them in most other settings is that in action learning, questions seek not only answers. Rather, they seek to go deeper, to understand, to respond to what is being asked, to give it thought. Questions are not a quest for solutions, they are an opportunity to explore.

Asking questions rather than immediately providing solutions unfreezes the group and defuses defensiveness. When one gives advice or answers immediately to a person, it makes that individual defensive ("you must think I'm dumb not to have thought of that solution") or the group becomes boxed in (reaching a conclusion without having the context, the systems-based causes for this problem).

Questions open up the problem—they make it a group problem, not just your problem. Individuals are much more conducive to questions because they allow one to give answers and thereby have some knowledge and power that will be of value to

eventually solving the problem. "You should have handled the problem this way," creates defensiveness much more than "Have you considered handling the problem this way?" The ability to ask the right questions when everything is uncertain and nobody knows what to do next is when out-of-box creativeness emerges.

Helpful and challenging questions are key to successful action learning groups. Asking questions causes people to think—provided they are asked in the supportive, sharing spirit. Helpful questions are those that open doors in the mind, get people to think more deeply, test their assumptions, explore why they do things, and what stops them.

What exactly are the helpful, "right" questions? The right questions are simply those that, when asked at the right time, give you the information you need. If you fail to come up with the right questions for a given project, you won't get the information you need to solve the problem.

What questions do for you:

- help clarify ("Are you saying that?")

- attempt to understand ("Could you explain more?")

- open up new avenues ("Have you thought of?")

- unpeel layers ("And then what happened?")

- offer ideas and insights ("Would such and such help?")

Questions help "unpack" a statement and challenge as well as offer insights, ideas, and suggestions.

During the beginning phases of an action learning set, six key questions are often asked. The first three questions can help identify underlying assumptions and expectations:

1. What is the organization (are we, are you) seeking to accomplish?

2. What is stopping the organization (us, you) from accomplishing it?

3. What can the organization (we, you) do about it?

The next three questions help the group focus on the realities of the situation:

4. Who knows what we are trying to do (who has the real facts and can put things into a proper perspective)?

5. Who cares about getting it implemented (who has a vested interest in getting the problem solved as opposed to merely talking about it)?

6. Who can get it implemented (who has the power; who controls the resources that can make change happen)?

These six questions always lead to more questions, and generally to even more discriminating questions. As one hears him or herself respond to questions, certain inconsistencies may become apparent; alternatively, talking out loud can lead to presenters developing insight, ideas, or explanations that had not occurred to them while going over the issue in their own mind. The very act of talking aloud is often creative.

Moreover, it is not only the responder who benefits from the questioning process. As set members ask questions—and see themselves being seriously considered—it gives them confidence in themselves and their ability to ask effective and relevant questions, which in turn, results in them beginning to behave differently at work.

Also, as group members are asked questions, they are pulled back or propelled forward into a higher level of reflective listening. This reflection is crucial to solving the problem and helping individuals and groups learn. It make us more aware of ourselves and what is happening around us.

Action learning programs provide the essential time and space to stand back and reflect, to unfreeze thoughts, to rise above everyday problems, to bring things into perspective, and to listen so as to draw out the experience and practical judgment of the group members. This questioning-reflection process also encourages the viewing of each other as learning resources.

In action learning, members should be open to try out new ways of doing things, to experiment, to reflect on experiences, to consider the results or effects of the experience, and to repeat the cycle by trying out new knowledge in different situations.

The heart of action learning is the process of reflection. It is designed to develop questioning insight, or as Revans states, "the capacity to ask fresh questions in conditions of ignorance, risk, and confusion, when nobody knows what to do next."

Commitment to Action

For action learning advocates, there is no real learning unless action is taken—and no action should occur without learning from it. Therefore, members of any action learning group must have the power to take action themselves or be assured that their recommendations will be implemented (barring any significant change in the environment or the group's obvious lack of essential information). Action enhances learning because it provides a basis and anchor for the critical dimension of reflection described earlier.

Action learning, therefore, requires action to be taken, not merely the presentation of recommendations. Implementation is part of the contract between the organization and the action learning group; thus the action learning formula can be expanded to $L = P + Q + R + I$. After learning about supervision before entering the group, raising questions, and engaging in self-reflection, people decide to act differently after returning to their jobs. They supervise employees differently and see how much more effective it is and continue to use that method or, if it did not work well, not use it again.

Action learning groups should have the expectation and responsibility of carrying out their ideas and recommendations. Merely preparing reports and recommendations for someone else to work out results in diminished commitment, effectiveness, and learning on the part of group members. Being required to implement, however, prevents the group from resembling a think tank or a debating group. As intellectually stimulating and emotionally venting as such groups might be, without implementation nothing actually changes.

Action Learning and Learning Organizations

Perhaps no tool is more effective in building a learning organization than action learning. Lex Dilworth has called action learning "the DNA of a learning organization," since action learning enables and forces organizations to continuously learn on a organization-wide basis and, thereby, able to adapt to a continuously changing environment.

There are many elements of action learning that contribute to the building of a learning organization—it helps an organization move from a culture of training to a culture of learning where everyone is responsible for their own continuous learning. Specifically, action learning:

- is outcome oriented

- systematically transfers knowledge

- enables people to learn by doing

- helps develop how-to learning skills

- encourages continual learning

- creates a learning culture; learning becomes a way of life

- is an active rather than a passive approach

- is done mainly on the job rather than off the job

- allows for mistakes and experimentation

- develops skills of critical reflection and reframing

- develops learning skills and behavior

- demonstrates the benefits of organizational learning

- models working and learning simultaneously

- is problem focused rather than hierarchically bound

- provides a network for sharing, supporting, and feedback

- challenges assumptions

- develops ability to generate information

- breaks down barriers across traditional boundaries

- is system based

- is applied to other, appropriate parts of the organization

Unless the organization, group, or individual enacts the projects and tasks, there is no evidence that something different or better has or can be done and consequently, no indication exists whether any learning or development has taken place. Only testing the group's ideas will enable the action set to determine whether their ideas are effective and practical, whether any issues have been overlooked, what problems occur as a result, how to tackle them, what to do differently in the future, and how they can be applied to other parts of the organization.

Commitment to Learning

Solving an organizational problem provides immediate, short-term benefits to an organization. The greater, longer-term, multiplier benefit is the learning gained by the group members and how their learnings can be applied on a systems-wide basis throughout the organization.

Therefore, during the action learning process, individuals take responsibility for their own, the team's, and the organization's learning and development. Time is set aside to talk about personal learnings and how the team's learning can be utilized in other parts of the organization.

The process results in powerful, significant learning due to its adherence to a number of key learning principles:

- Learning is increased when we reflect on what we did in the experience.

- Greater learning occurs when given time and space, and when a sense of urgency exists.

- We can see results when we are allowed to take risks and when we are encouraged and supported in our deliberations.

- We can learn critically when we are able to question the assumptions on which our actions are based.

- We learn when we receive accurate feedback from others and from the results of our problem-solving actions.

- When relying solely on experts, we often become immobilized and do not seek or trust our own solutions.

- Nonhierarchical groups from across organizational departments and functions are often better able to gain new perspectives and therefore augment the learning.

- Action learning is most effective when the learners are examining the organizational system as a whole.

- Group responsibility for the task to be tackled empowers the members and enhances learning.

We are most challenged when we work on unfamiliar problems in unfamiliar settings—this is where the greatest learning may occur. As we work in unfamiliar areas, we unfreeze some of our previous ways of doing things and develop new ways of thinking. By working cooperatively with others on real issues, the projects force the members to move to higher levels of learning relative to application, synthesis, and evaluation.

Action learning is built on the entire learning cycle: Learning and creating knowledge through concrete experience, observing and reflecting on this experience, forming generalizations from experiences and testing the implications of those generalizations in new experiences, and beginning the process again.

Group Facilitation

The group facilitator or set advisor may be a working group member who is familiar with the problem being discussed, or an external participant who does not necessarily understand the problem content or organizational context, but possesses action learning facilitation skills.

The facilitator is very important in helping participants reflect both on what they are learning and how they are solving problems. This individual helps group members reflect on how they listen, how they may have reframed the problem, how they give each other feedback, how they are planning and working, and what assumptions may be shaping their beliefs and actions. The set advisor also helps participants focus on what they are achieving, what they are finding difficult, what processes they are employing, and the implications of these processes.

The set advisor may use a variety of means to capture the learning of the members. The group may be asked to reflect on what and how they are learning, their interactions, and applications. The facilitator may intervene during the problem-solving process or may arrange a time at the end of each meeting for members to reflect on what they have learned.

The set advisor should be trained in and understand how his or her actions can assist the action learning process. This person should be competent and confident working with the processes that are basic to action learning: airspace (talking time) for every member, a focus on the task or projects in hand, a questioning approach, attention to listening, time for reflection, emphasis on learning, and avoidance of judgment.

Types of Action Learning Programs

Essentially there are two basic types of action learning programs: single-project, in-company programs and multiple-task, open-set programs.

Single-Project Programs

In this type of action learning program, the organization establishes one or more action learning sets to solve specific problems or resolve particular challenges of the organization. The learning set acts as a resource group that works on a single, common issue within an organization.

These action learning programs have a "client"— someone who understands the nature of the program, thinks it is important, and can be influential in making sure the group can gain access to whomever or whatever information they require. The client—who may or may not be an actual member of the set—assures that the program is given high visibility and acceptance. This person is seen as the "champion" of the action learning program.

Precisely who will be members of the group depends on the program goals. The participants may be chosen by management or they may be volunteers. If the project is a companywide initiative—such as corporate strategy or creating a new corporate culture— a large cross-section of staff is likely to be involved. If, however, the issue is more focused— such as creating a new staff appraisal system—participants may be selected according to their interest and knowledge.

Single-project programs generally go through the following phases:

Introductory period during which the action learning set explores the questions of "what we are trying to do, what is preventing us, and how can we overcome those obstacles?"

Diagnostic period where the issues of "who knows," "who cares," and "who can" are examined.

Cigna International Property and Casualty Corporation

At the Philadelphia, Pennsylvania, headquarters of Cigna, action learning groups are composed of a diverse range of individuals—employees from numerous departments and holding various positions, as well as Cigna's clients. To meet the insurance company criteria, people are placed in action learning groups that work 40 hours a week for four to five weeks. Each group is assigned a single problem facing one of Cigna's divisions. One or two members of the action learning set hail from the division facing the problem while all other divisions send one or two individuals to participate in the group.

One such action learning set was charged with evaluating the business strategy of a segment of the company that was losing money. Their purpose was to determine whether the business's current strategy was a viable one.

In the first week, the group was immersed in absorbing a lot of data about the business problem, as well as data on strategy and how to apply theory to strategy. Later, group members went into the field and interviewed customers, competitors, and employees in order to determine the

soundness of the current strategy. The third and fourth weeks were spent assimilating the data and then presenting an action plan.

Cigna management was so pleased with the learning group's results that it immediately, and successfully, implemented the group's action plan.

The Action Learning Cycle

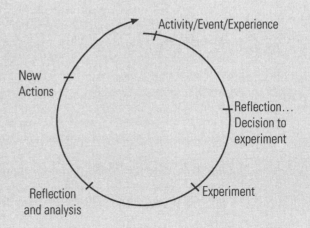

Consultation period in which outside resources are interviewed or observed.

Implementation period during which action plans are developed, recommended to senior management, and implemented.

Review period in which learning is shared and project solutions are applied systematically to other parts of the organization.

The special advantages of a single-project, in-company action learning set are:

- networking and interdepartmental contacts are created

- visibility such a program gives group members

- greater cohesiveness within an organization as people

- realizing the benefits of working together

Open-Set, Multiple-Task Action Learning Programs

An open set is one in which each individual member brings his or her own project, task, or problem to the table. Each person is a client for the other group members. The set members support and assist each other for an agreed-upon period of time. Usually all the set members are from different organizations, although the group may be comprised of people from different units of the same organization.

The process in an open set works as follows:

■ *Step 1*
Four to eight people meet on a periodic basis to work and learn together. Set members act as a resource to one another. They support and challenge each other as they tackle their allotted project and focus on learning.

■ *Step 2*
The time ("airspace") is divided among the set members for each to present his or her problem to the rest of the group, explain what work has been done since the last meeting, what the results were, what new difficulties have arisen, and what further action he or she intends to take. The rest of the group serve as questioners, consultants, and advisors.

■ *Step 3*
At the end of his or her allocated time, the presenter offers up a commitment as to what will be achieved before the next meeting.

■ *Step 4*
Members may rotate serving in the set advisor role or the group may seek an external set advisor.

Some unique advantages of open set are:

Broader vision. Group members are able to see how different organizations tackle the same issues and problems. (Recognizing that people in different companies tend to have different perspectives, values, and understanding. Just hearing them is valuable as it challenges one's preconceived notions that things have to be a certain way).

Openness of discussion. Members have more freedom to discuss issues as one tends to be more open and honest with people who are not working in one's organization.

No hierarchical restrictions. There are fewer hierarchical relationships and issues to be concerned about. There is the opportunity of sharing with peers.

Establishing Programs in a Company

The typical sequence of activities for an organization to establish action learning teams is as follows:

1. An organization-wide workshop is conducted to ensure that managers and workers understand how action learning works. External action learning consultants or staff trained in action learning explain and demonstrate the basic principles and dynamics of action learning.

2. A project or projects are identified for action learning sets. The project chosen should be meaningful to participants as it relates to their jobs as well as important to the organization as a whole. Projects should also be ones for which employees could offer several viable solutions, rather than problems which could better be solved by an expert.

3. Action learning teams are formed with four to eight people from diverse backgrounds and functional expertise. This diversity enables the learning teams to examine the problems from a fresh and different perspective. A facilitator may also be assigned to be part of the team, although this is not a requirement. The facilitator is preferably someone whom the team members are not acquainted with so that he or she can act independently of the group's culture.

4. The action learning teams meet on a periodic basis (daily, weekly, bi-weekly) over a period of a few weeks to several months. The group meets for a full day or a few hours depending upon the nature of the problems and the time constraints of its members. Learning is developed around the discussion and resolution of each project. This may include feedback, reflective analysis, and brainstorming.

5. After the project is completed, the facilitator helps group members conduct a final reflection on their work in order to learn more about how they identified, assessed, and solved problems; what increased their learning; how they communicated; and what assumptions shaped their actions.

Action learning programs need not be organization-wide. They can begin in one part and later be filtered throughout the organization, thus becoming a catalyst for change and learning. Action learning programs can begin wherever significant learning is possible and needed.

Benefits of Action Learning

Action learning can be a most valuable vehicle for resolving an organization's most crucial problems, for applying learning throughout the organization, and for building a vigorous learning organization. It can rapidly develop critical skills needed by individuals and teams in today's work environment. Action learning has indeed become one of the most valuable tools now used by world-class companies as they leap into the 21st century.

Potential Pitfalls and How To Avoid Them

There are a number of factors that can make action learning ineffective for problem solving and organizational learning.

■ *Inappropriate Choice of Project*
Make sure the project lies within the authority and scope of responsibility of the participants. The project should be neither so large as to swamp the team, nor too small or simple to make the project useless. Always remember, it should be a problem and not a puzzle.

■ *Lack of Support from Top Management*
Make sure senior management support the program and its participants. It can be demoralizing for a group to work very hard and long at solving a problem only to have their ideas rejected by an unsympathetic, inflexible leadership.

■ *Lack of Time*
There has to be sufficient time allocated for the project to go from incubation through to implementation. Make sure there is time for reflection and learning during the meetings.

■ *Poor Mix of Participants*
Make sure that there are members who are familiar with the problem, but also include those who bring fresh perspectives to the table.

■ *Lack of Commitment by Participants*
Make sure participants are aware that it is in their own and the company's interest to commit to the program; they should own the problem and care about the results.

■ *All Action and No Learning*
Ensure that emphasis is on learning and not just on action. This maximizes long-term organizational benefits.

■ *Incompetent Set Advisor*
Use only trained set advisors. Without adequate preparation, you cannot turn a line manager or even a trainer into a competent set advisor.

References & Resources

Articles

Beaty, Liz, et al. "Action Learning: Reflections on Becoming a Set Member." *Management Education & Development,* vol. 24, no. 4, 1993, pp. 350-367.

Bencivenga, Dominic. "Learning Organizations Evolve in a New Direction." *HR Magazine,* November 1995, pp. 69-73.

Boddy, David. "Putting Action Learning into Practice." *Journal of European Industrial Training,* vol. 5, no. 5, 1981, pp. 2-20.

Dixon, Nancy. "Action Learning, Action Science and Learning New Skills." *Industrial and Commercial Training,* vol. 22, no. 4 1990, pp. 1-17.

Donaghue, Charles. "Towards a Model of Set Advisor Effectiveness." *Journal of European Industrial Training,* vol. 16, no. 1, 1992.

Froiland, Paul. "Action Learning: Taming Real Problems in Real Time." *Training,* January 1994, pp. 27-34.

Gayeski, Diane M. "From 'Training Department' to 'Learning Organization.'" *Performance Improvement,* vol. 35, no. 7, 1996, pp. 8-11.

Gephart, Martha A., et al. "Learning Organizations Come Alive." *Training & Development,* December 1996, pp. 34-45.

Margerison, Charles. "Action Learning and Excellence in Management Development." *Journal of Management Studies,* vol. 32, no. 5, 1988, pp. 43-53.

Marquardt, Michael. "Action Learning: Foundation for Organizational Learning and Corporate Success" *Training & Development in Australia,* November 1996, pp. 7-12.

Marsick, Victoria, et al., "Action-Reflection Learning." *Training & Development,* August 1992, pp. 63-66.

Mumford, Alan (ed.). "Action Learning Special Issue." *Journal of Management Development,* vol 6, no. 2, 1987.

Mumford, Alan. "Learning in Action." *Personnel Management,* July 1991, pp. 34-37.

Oliver, Carol, et al. "Who Cross-fertilizes Most on MBA Programs?" *Industrial and Commercial Training,* vol. 23, no. 3, 1991, pp. 8-14.

Peters, John, and Peter Smith. "Developing High-Potential Staff—An Action Learning Approach." *Employee Counselling Today,* vol. 8, no. 3, 1995.

Prideaux, G. "Making Action Learning More Effective." *Training and Management Development Methods,* vol. 6, 1992.

Revans, Reginald. "What is Action Learning?" *Journal of Management Development,* vol. 1, no. 3, 1982, pp. 64-75.

Sims, Ronald R. "The Enhancement of Learning in Public Sector Training Programmes." *Public Personnel Management,* vol. 22, no. 2, 1993, p. 243.

Smith, David. "Company Based Projects: Using Action Learning to Develop Consultancy Skills." *Journal of Management Development,* vol. 11, no. 1, 1992.

Sorohan, E. Gordan. "We Do: Therefore, We Learn." *Training & Development,* vol. 47, no. 10, 1993, pp. 47-52.

Wishart, Nicole A., et al. "Redrawing the Portrait of a Learning Organization." *Academy of Management Executive,* vol. 10, no. 1, 1996, pp. 7-20.

Books

Boude D., et al. (eds.). *Reflection: Turning Experience into Learning.* London: Kogan Page, 1985.

Chawla, Sarita, and John Renesch (eds.). *Learning Organizations: Developing Cultures for Tomorrow's Workplace.* Portland, Oregon: Productivity Press, 1995.

Inglis, Scott. *Making the Most of Action Learning.* Brookfield, Vermont: Gower Publishing, 1994.

Mai, Robert P. *Learning Partnerships: How Leading American Companies Implement Organizational Learning.* Alexandria, Virginia: American Society for Training & Development.

Marquardt, Michael J. *Building the Learning Organization: A Systems Approach to Quantum Improvement and Global Success.* New York: McGraw-Hill, 1996.

Marquardt, Michael J., and Angus Reynolds. *The Global Learning Organization: Gaining Competitive Advantage Through Continuous Learning.* Burr Ridge, Illinois: Irwin Professional Publishing, 1994.

McGill, Ian., and L. Beatty. *Action Learning: A Practitioner's Guide.* London: Kogan Page, 1992.

Mumford, Alan (ed.). *Insights into Action Learning.* Bradford, England: MCB University Press, 1984.

Pedler, Michael. *Action Learning for Managers.* London: Lemos & Crane, 1996.

Pedler, Michael (ed.). *Action Learning in Practice.* Brookfield, Vermont: Gower Publishing, 1991.

Revans, Reginald. *The ABC of Action Learning.* Bromley, England: Chartwell-Brat, 1982.

Revans, Reginald. *The Origins and Growth of Action Learning.* Bromley, England: Chartwell-Bratt, 1982.

Senge, Peter. *The Fifth Discipline: The Art and Practice of the Learning Organization.* New York: Doubleday, 1990.

Watkins, Karen E., and Victoria J. Marsick (eds.). *Creating the Learning Organization.* Alexandria, Virginia: American Society for Training & Development, 1996.

Weinstein, Krystyna. *Action Learning: A Journey in Discovery and Development.* London: HarperCollins, 1995.

Wills, Gordon. *Your Enterprise School of Management.* Bradford, England: MCB University Press, 1993.

Info-lines

Marquardt, Michael. "16 Steps to Becoming a Learning Organization." No. 9602 (updated 1997).

Zulauf, Carol Ann. "Systems Thinking." No. 9703.

Internet Resources

http://www.imc.org.uk/imc/al-inter/home.htm

http://www.mcb.co.uk/services/coursewa/mba/imb1.htm

http://www.imc.org.uk/imc/apc-1996/papers/ali-news.htm

http://copper.ucs.indiana.edu/~ciyang/page1.html

http://www.imc.org.uk/services/coursewa/benefits/file4.htm

http://www.tlainc.com/index2.htm

http://freenet.vcu.edu/civic/organ/act-learn/actfaq.html

http://www.gil.com.au/comm/alarpm/singbr~1.htm

http://members.aol.com/Littlerv/index.html

http://www.swin.edu.au/nsdi/action.html

http://www.wa.gov.au/sbi/tots/action.html

http://arch.hku.hk/research/ALP/ALP.html

Effective Action Learning Checklist

Use the following checklist for putting an effective action learning program together for your organization.

Step 1:
Preparing for Action Learning Programs

Orientation for the Organization

☐ Does everyone understand the nature and purpose of action learning programs?

☐ Is there agreement on overall objectives for the program?

☐ Is management committed to the program? Are there champions for the action learning sets?

☐ Has the program and its objectives been discussed with potential participants and their managers?

☐ Do managers and participants understand the time factor involved?

Projects

☐ Do the projects meet the organization's needs as well as provide learning opportunities?

☐ Are they problems rather than puzzles?

☐ Are the projects feasible and manageable?

☐ Will the group have the authority to implement their recommendations? Or will they first need to be presented to higher management for implementation?

☐ Who will be the client for the group?

Participants

☐ Have group members been carefully selected (members can be chosen by their managers, self-selected, or by an individual who has a stake in solving the problem)?

☐ Is there an appropriate member mix to provide fresh perspectives, and knowledge?

☐ Have set advisors been chosen and trained?

Step 2:
Start-Up Workshop

☐ Has a training workshop been developed that assures that the participants will have:

☐ Gained an understanding of the basic concepts and mechanics of action learning?

☐ Agreed with the client on the problem/task?

☐ Identified resources (contacts) that may be needed?

Step 3:
First Set Meetings

☐ Have set members agreed to adopt action learning processes relative to airspace, asking questions, and reflection?

☐ Have they agreed on future dates for set meetings and committed to attend regularly?

☐ Have they identified a place convenient for participants—preferably away from the workplace (to avoid interruptions)?

☐ Are action learning processes observed at all meetings unless set decides otherwise?

Step 4:
Final Wrap-up Meeting

☐ Has there been a review of the learning?

☐ Has a systematic analysis of how the learning can be applied to other parts of the organization occurred?

☐ Have verbal or written reports been prepared for the clients, managers, and others interested?

The material appearing on this page is not covered by copyright and may be reproduced at will.

Chaos and Complexity Theory

issue 9807

Chaos and Complexity Theory

A U T H O R :

T. J. Titcomb

35 Brandt Boulevard
Landisville, PA 17538
Tel: 717.898.1635
E-mail: TJTtCOMB@aol.com

T.J. Titcomb has been a trainer, management consultant, and therapist for more than 20 years. She is Director of Training & Consultation for Workplace Solutions, a division of Family Service, Lancaster, Pennsylvania. T.J. is working on her Ph.D. in Organizational Development at Temple University.

Editor
Cat Sharpe

Associate Editor
Sabrina E. Hicks

Production Design
Anne Morgan

ASTD Internal Consultant
Phil Anderson

Chaos and Complexity Theory

Traditionally, managers learn that the "right" way of supervising employees involves careful planning, coordination, and control. In reality, however, management behavior is unplanned, random, and contingent. In today's fast-changing and competitive work environment, plans often derail and managers have less time to coordinate and control the actions of their employees. For this reason, chaos and complexity theory is applicable to organizations.

More than 20 years ago, chaos and complexity theory began to take shape in the scientific world. A critical leap occurred in 1977 at the University of California, Santa Cruz, when a group of doctoral students began exploring the ways in which order emerges from chaos. Borrowing theories that physicists and mathematicians had been exploring for decades, they discovered that the universe is a vibrant and chaotic system, not a static machine subject to our control. As their research progressed, the students determined that, while the universe and other systems are extremely complex, they contain patterns that can lead to a greater understanding of their structure and an ability to predict patterns that they will follow.

How does chaos and complexity theory translate into good organizational management? How and why would someone want to apply these scientific theories to business organizations? The reason is this: Since the introduction of the Aristotelian/ Ptolemaic System (which first presented a controlled order for the planets), humans have attempted to find order in their environment.

Today, we continue this struggle for order in the way we manage our business organizations. We want to create organizational charts: We want to place everyone in a box and line-up these boxes in a linear and hierarchical fashion. With the surge of this new science, and our knowledge that scientific theories historically progress into the science of business, organizations that apply the basic principles involved in chaos and complexity theory can learn to exploit their environment and co-evolve with other "chaotic" organizations in the 21st century.

This *Info-line* will define chaos and complexity theory and apply this theory to business management. By describing the characteristics of chaos and complexity theory found in organizations and providing a glossary of terms, this issue provides a loose guideline for how to apply chaos and complexity theory to your organization. Additionally, this *Info-line* describes the pros and cons of applying this theory and concludes by describing the implications on trainers.

But remember, this is only a basic introduction to chaos and complexity theory. Use it to get an understanding of the basic principles behind this theory before you delve into the scientific details.

Defining Simple/Complex Systems

Just what are chaos and complexity anyway? Answers vary depending on the person providing the definition. Purists would criticize combining the terms because they represent distinct theories from different disciplines. Some explain the difference between the two by saying *chaos* is the study of how simple systems can generate complicated behavior while *complexity* is the study of how complicated systems generate simple behavior.

Simple Systems

For a system to be simple, it must be linear and have little or no interaction with other systems. Simple systems have order and will not present you with any surprises. For example, if you were to drop an apple from the top of an 10-story building down to the paved parking lot below, the apple would fall to the ground and smash upon impact.

If a change is introduced to a simple system, you can easily predict the outcome that this change will excite. In the example above, let the apple fall into a huge bucket of water instead of a paved parking lot. It is easy to predict that the apple will, this time, survive the fall.

Glossary

Before you can begin to understand chaos and complexity, you will need to understand some of the terms and phrases associated with them. This glossary will get you started.

Attractor: A point or region that a system is drawn toward. A *strange attractor* reveals an orderly pattern to apparent chaos. In the graphic images produced by non-linear equations, lines never go through the same point twice, yet they remain within certain bounds, seemingly pulled by the attractor.

Bifurcation Point: A moment of change, a fork in the road. Systems are very sensitive to small fluctuations that can change their path at this point; thus, predicting the outcome is impossible.

Butterfly Effect: The often-quoted metaphor that an action as minute as the flap of a butterfly's wings can lead to large or even catastrophic effects in a distant area. Complex systems are extremely sensitive to initial differences that become magnified as the system changes.

Chaos: The study of behavior in systems that appears random but reveals orderly patterns at deeper levels. In a business sense, it describes random, inherently unpredictable sequences over time in the performance indicators of an organization.

Complexity: Consisting of interconnected or interwoven parts. Dynamic complexity exists in situations where cause and effect are subtle and effects over time are not obvious.

Dissipative Structures: Complex structures that survive by taking in and giving off energy. When new information coming into the system creates enough disturbance, the system transforms itself to a new form.

Equilibrium: A state in which there is no tendency to move away from a given behavior pattern.

Far From Equilibrium: A state in which behavior is easily changed to a qualitatively different form by small-chance disturbances. It implies disorder, instability, chaos, and fractal behavior.

Fractal: Patterns that repeat at different levels in complex systems (that is, self-similarity across scale). Fractal dimension measures the constant degree of irregularity in a chaotic pattern. The term is also used for the geometric figures (such as, the Mandelbrot set) generated by nonlinear equations to illustrate the principle.

Phase Transition: The point at which an element changes form (such as, water boiling and becoming steam). These can be major turning points for organizations when change is sudden and discontinuous. See "bifurcation point."

Self-Organization: A process in which changes in system structure and behavior appear spontaneously as the need arises. According to Margaret Wheatley, these changes are "always consistent with what has gone on before, with the history and identity of the system" because self reference is "fundamental to self-organizing systems."

Sensitivity to Initial Conditions: The amplifying property of non-linear feedback mechanisms (which means, tiny changes can escalate to totally change long-term behavior). See "butterfly effect."

System: A combination of parts that function as an integrated whole. The relationships and connections between the parts are essential properties of the system.

Complex Systems

If complexity is the study of how complicated systems generate simple behavior, what is a complex system? Most people think of complex systems as those that have many different parts—like a jig saw puzzle—but that is merely complexity of detail. A complex system is a system that is nonlinear and interactive. When discussing complex systems, Francis Heylighen, a noted researcher of the evolutionary development of higher levels of complexity at the Free University of Brussels, defines complex as a system that has "two or more components [that] are joined in such a way that it is difficult to separate them."

Perhaps the best way to define a complex system is to provide a tangible example. One of the most complex systems is the human brain. Our brains contain over 100 billion nerve cells and the connections between the individual cells are even more important and numerous than the cells themselves. While every brain is different, each one has the responsibility to process its owner's perceptions and control the operations and interactions of the body's organs.

The type of complex systems that applies to organizations is dynamic complexity. Here, the elements in a system can relate to each other in many different ways. In addition, as the state of each element changes, its relationships with other elements change. This change in the relationship produces yet another change—a change in the corresponding elements.

A popular metaphor for complexity theory—*the butterfly effect*—illustrates how these small changes in an individual element can have profound effects on the entire organization (which scientists refer to as *sensitive dependence on initial conditions*). A butterfly flaps its wings in the South American jungle, altering the path of the wind slightly, which in turn shifts global wind patterns, ultimately creating tornadoes in Kansas.

Even systems with few parts can be complex. In a family or small team, for example, each person's health or mood can have profound effects on the other members. This changes the way that person reacts with other individuals as well as the entire group dynamic.

Applying Science to Management

As research into chaos and complexity theory has become more widespread, organizational experts have found that organizations are near perfect examples of complex, nonlinear dynamic systems—phenomena usually studied by theoretical physicists, mathematicians, and biologists. In fact, members of the Chaos Think Tank have gone as far as to suggest that chaos is "the" science of management:

Chaos is the *science of complex, dynamical, nonlinear systems. Organizations are complex, dynamical, nonlinear systems. Therefore, chaos is* the *science of organization . . . the* new *science of management.*

To apply chaos and complexity theory to organizational management, learning organization expert Mike McMasters has developed the following applicable definitions:

Chaos is a state where patterns cannot be made nor details understood. Chaos is the result of an organization resisting change and then reaching a point where change is unavoidable. At this point, change occurs rapidly and can take a system in unexpected directions. Eventually, the system either reorganizes itself in a viable state or disintegrates.

Complex systems have details, whose role in the larger system cannot be understood fully by examining them apart from the system. By carefully studying the whole system, patterns can be identified.

Additionally, we can see specific elements of chaos and complexity theory in organizations, such as the butterfly effect. Take, for example, a manufacturing environment. At John Deere's seed planter facility (see the case study on the following page), an individual on the wheel team is unable to install tires fast enough. This causes that team to not feed wheels into the production line fast enough, which in turn causes a bottleneck. This *one individual* on *one team* sends ripples throughout the entire organization, causing a dramatic change in its ability to achieve organizational goals.

Case Study: John Deere

With the various planter sizes and options available at the John Deere manufacturing facility, one production line can make more than one million possible combinations. In attempt to streamline the process, management assigned each self-directed work team one element of the product as their domain. As you might imagine, however, scheduling all of these teams to eliminate bottlenecks and comply with production schedules was a nightmare. With incentive pay at stake, teams were fighting among themselves, and the scheduling department was spending an inordinate amount of time compiling scheduling spreadsheets in a seemingly futile attempt to smooth the production and delivery processes.

The solution to their problem came from Bill Fulkerson, a staff analyst at Deere familiar with complexity theory. He looked at complex genetic systems and noticed that, as species reproduce, those with the best characteristics have a better chance of reproducing. This gradually reduces the number of bad characteristics in the population. Fulkerson realized that the same principles could be applied to creating a more efficient schedule. He contracted with Bolt, Beranek, and Newman, Inc., who previously had used genetic algorithms to schedule work at Navy labs, to produce a similar system for Deere.

Now, a single computer on the shop floor is fed information each evening and left overnight to "breed" more than 600,000 schedules. As schedules are created and breed with each other, those with the best characteristics survive to combine with others—less desirable schedules "die." In the morning, the best possible schedule is ready to be implemented, without staff having to create it. As a result, production and delivery schedules are more efficient and overtime has nearly vanished.

To solve this manufacturing problem, John Deere choose to use an organic planning program. This program allows them to analyze the myriad ways in which teams and individuals work together to account for various work speeds. John Deere can then "breed" the most efficient schedule possible to coordinate everyone's efforts—eliminating the bottleneck.

Characteristics of Complex Systems

Complex systems, like John Deere's planter facility, all share certain characteristics—it does not matter if they relate to the physical world or to organizations. Although theorists do not agree on which characteristics are most important, most accept the following as a central part of chaos and complexity theory.

■ *The Whole Is More Than the Parts*

Traditionally, we learn that the best way to understand a complex system is to break it down into smaller, more manageable chunks. If you examine a system one component at a time, you cannot see how each component interacts with other components, much less see how everything works together. As a result, vital information is not readily apparent.

For example, if you analyze only one note of a symphony, can you understand the symphony as a whole? Of course not. Likewise, by examining the role of team members as individuals—and nothing else, you are unable to see how the members interact and how the team functions as a whole.

Here is another example. Take a familiar poem or saying, write each word of the poem on a separate piece of paper, and mix all the pieces of paper in a hat. Knowing that all of the elements of the system (that is, the poem) are present, assemble the words in an order that has meaning. After you complete this exercise, examine how the poem derives its meaning from the way the pieces fit together and interact with one another. The meaning of a system comes from how the pieces are connected.

■ *Patterns Appear Throughout the System*

All complex systems are made up of a limited number of repeating patterns. Although they may appear to occur randomly, look closely and you can see that certain behaviors and qualities begin to appear again and again. In business, you can observe echoes of common actions and attitudes in members on different levels and at different parts of an organization. Even when the system changes, these actions and attitudes stay within certain invisible boundaries.

Take, for example, a head of broccoli. If you break the head into sections, each section resembles a miniature version of the whole. This is true even if you break it down into individual stalks. In organizations, this can lead to a sense of *deja vu,* the feeling that you have experienced something before. Everyday on the job is different, yet eventually you notice that the same kinds of behavior, issues, and problems crop up again and again.

■ *Cause and Effect Is Never Simple*

It can be difficult to determine whether one action caused another to occur. Most events in complex systems have multiple causes that you cannot always closely linked in time and space; thus, if you were to isolate one action and examine it, you may make inaccurate perceptions. For example, if you watched one fish swerve in response to the approach of another fish, you might assume that the first fish was responding only to the approach of the other one. If you were to pan back and look at the entire school, however, you would see that the first fish's actions were influenced by—and part of—a complex system in which each member of the school acts to keep the school together and moving in the same direction.

Inaccurate assumptions like this also occur in organizations. Work groups often have a "problem person": someone who is subtly or overtly blamed for conflicts and difficulties within the group. If you observe this individual interacting with only one or two other group members, you may come to the conclusion that the blame is well placed. When this "problem" leaves the group, however, often another person assumes this role. If you stop observing the individual and begin to observe the group as a whole, you should be able to determine why the group *needs* to have a problem person.

The Santa Fe Institute

The Santa Fe Institute (SFI) is a private, non-profit, multidisciplinary research and education center founded in 1984. Since its establishment, SFI has been devoted to creating a new kind of scientific research community that pursues emerging science. Operating as a small visiting institution, SFI draws scientists from universities and research institutions around the world to pursue a wide range of problems. Most of their work focuses on the science of complexity, with researchers working on projects that range from the communication patterns of ants to the way information spreads across global markets. The goal for all of these projects is to shed light on problems that challenge our global society and to encourage the practical applications of the results.

Many of the complex systems under study at SFI share a common self-organizing architecture. This architecture consists of a noncentralized (distributed) collection of autonomous "agents." These agents interact in the context of a dynamic environment, and the focus is on the coupling between individual and global behaviors.

Currently, SFI is conducting research on the Swarm simulation system, developed by Christopher Langton to study complex systems. The simulator was designed to study the collective behavior of organisms, such as finding food or flying in a pattern. It can also model the behavior of complex human systems.

In recent years, a new view of learning and learning-based systems has emerged. Researchers have found that the study (and design) of complex, open-ended learning environments requires a framework in which intelligence is shared among multiple agents interacting with each other and their environment. The evolution of researchers at SFI drives changes in its research programs as collaborations grow, mutate, join other groups, or eventually die out as interest in the scientific community changes. In this way, SFI not only studies complex systems, it is itself a model of a successful complex system that other organizations can study and emulate.

■ *History Does and Doesn't Repeat Itself*

Although patterns appear throughout systems, subtle differences emerge each time a pattern is repeated. Patterns may *seem* to be identical, but complex systems are "aperiodic"—they never repeat in *exactly* the same way. You can never count on the same actions to produce exactly the same results. For example, if you were to give the same survey to the same group of people at various times, the responses you get would never be exactly the same. You could, however, predict the general pattern of the responses by analyzing past surveys given to that group.

■ *Change Comes from Chaos*

All systems constantly evolve. Some changes come smoothly; others are more disruptive. A system will resist change for as long as it can. While the system attempts to resist the change by keeping its current form, this change will continue to build pressure upon the system. This increasing instability throws the system into chaotic imbalance. At this point, sudden dramatic change will occur because the system will either re-invent itself to meet new challenges or disintegrate under the strain.

Take a balloon, for example. Inflate it, and the balloon expands to accommodate the added air. At a certain point, the added air places so much of a strain upon the balloon that it can no longer accommodate the increased volume, and it pops. While this chaotic imbalance can be just as traumatic for organizations as it is for the balloon, the system usually finds a new level of stability after adapting to the changes.

■ *The Future Can't and Can Be Predicted*

When dealing with complex systems, you can never be certain of the effect that an action will have on the entire system. Even the smallest differences get exaggerated over time—that is, small stones can create huge ripples throughout the system. While exact *quantitative* predictions are impossible, you can make relatively accurate guesses about the *qualitative* aspects of a system.

For example, when you conduct a training program, you can be reasonably certain that everyone learned at least some of what you were teaching. How much they remember and how well they apply that information back on the job cannot be predicted.

Complexity Theory

The central premise of complexity theory as it relates to organizations is that *order* can emerge out of *chaos*. The key for managers is to first develop a strong sense of vision in employees and to then step back and let the employees determine the detailed courses of action themselves. This vision should be strategic and contain a clear sense of the broader mission of your organization rather than stipulating specific paths. If you have instilled your vision properly and given your employees the tools and freedom to chart their own path, they will be able to choose the best course of action to reach the organization's goals. They will also be able to adapt to changing situations and improve processes as they discover new and better ways of doing their jobs.

A perfect example of this is the case study on termites (at far right), which can be easily adapted to human organizations. Employees should be free to discover and create "mounds" of activity consistent with the vision. Then, by creating a project or alliance with the potential to move the organization toward its goal, employees can generate enough interest that other employees "swarm" to their project. Projects that seem likely to succeed and move the organization toward its goal will attract both employees and resources, enabling it to continue. Projects that are perceived as inefficient or unlikely to succeed will not attract resources and will therefore "die" before they consume too much of peoples' time or the organization's money.

Johan Roos, in his paper "The Poised Organization: Navigating Effectively on Knowledge Landscapes" states that organizations who master complexity theory succeed because they perform the following tasks:

● know their identity

● explore and exploit their environment

- interact and co-evolve with other organizations

- study a relationship among its component parts

Using these tasks as group headings, Roos suggests that organizations pursue the following 10 strategies.

Identity

1. Recognize identity as the basis for the self-referencing essential to knowledge development.

2. Recognize that identity both provides tools to explore the possibilities for the organization and limits the organization's ability to see other paths.

3. Realize that the organization's identity can be shaped by external forces and will change accordingly. Resisting this change can damage the organization and lead to chaos.

Knowledge Development

4. Prioritize knowledge development, recognizing that the environment could change at any time.

5. Reflect on external factors that could require new knowledge or cause the organization to alter its path.

6. Develop knowledge by recognizing patterns rather than by attempting to guess what the future holds.

Co-Evolution

7. Develop knowledge through relationships, including strategic alliances, mergers, and acquisitions.

8. Form alliances that have at least some degree of regularity, a combination of chaos and stability.

Case Study: Termites

Tropical termites prove one of the best examples of a self-organizing system. Without any apparent central directing authority, they build huge colonies. The termites start by swarming over small mounds of dirt and building columns, seemingly at random. Once they reach a certain height, they stop building columns and then connect ones that are close together to form arches. Eventually, these mounds can reach heights of 10 feet, the equivalent to a human-constructed building over a mile high. How do they do it?

While no one knows for sure, scientists think that instinct, habit, and various forms of communication play a role. No matter how they coordinate their work, it is clear that there is no predetermined plan and that no one is in control. *Order* appears out of *chaos*. The termites' seemingly random, chaotic efforts are never exactly the same, but the overall *pattern* of termite mounds is always nearly the same. It appears that they follow a simple set of rules over and over until a livable mound takes shape, much the same way fractals are produced by repeating equations over and over. The rules that the termites follow could be as simple as the following:

- Find an elevated place.

- Build columns on it.

- Stop building after the column is twice as tall as you.

- If two columns are close together, close their tops to form an arch.

- Repeat.

From this example, managers can learn that you do not need to—and maybe shouldn't—direct every effort of your employees. By giving them a broad overview of what you hope to accomplish and a few simple instructions, you can set your employees free to reach their goal in the best way they can discover. Different teams may reach the goal in different ways, but the end result—the pattern—will be the same if you have carefully selected your vision and instructions. While this may lead to chaos initially, an organic, complex system will eventually evolve that will make the most efficient use of your resources.

(See the John Deere case study as an example of how human organizations apply these theories.)

Internal Relationships

9. Recognize and interpret the relationships among internal parts or agents as well as their relationships to the environment as a whole.

10. Seek a level of interconnectedness among the organization's component parts that reflect its environment and goals. Too much interconnectiveness can inhibit growth as much as too little.

Complexity and Your Organization

By adhering to strategies such as those listed above, organizations show how chaos and complexity theory focuses our attention on information and feedback mechanisms. These mechanisms bring us information that is essential to forming strategies and relationships both within and without the organization. In this way, it is quite similar to two accepted management practices: learning organizations and systems thinking.

The Learning Organization

Organizations that implement chaos and complexity theory share many of the characteristics of learning organizations. To adapt quickly to changing circumstances and "flock" resources around projects, organizations need to create an environment in which constant learning is a major part of its culture. Learning organizations accept the fact that nothing is completely stable and that they must be prepared to quickly change their strategies to adapt. Organizations can create and foster productive ways to learn through the following methods:

■ *Culture*
The culture of an organization includes its shared values, beliefs, assumptions, customs, and practices. Successful organizations realize that learning is an essential ingredient in success. They make learning a habit and integrate it into all organizational functions.

■ *Vision*
As mentioned earlier, organizations must develop a broad, clear vision of where they want to go. A desire for a future in which employees are encouraged to learn about and experiment with ways to deliver better products and services needs to be part of that vision.

■ *Strategy*
The tactics, methods, and action plans an organization uses to achieve its vision should include strategies for the collection, transferal, and use of knowledge in every area of the organization.

■ *Structure*
Organizations should be streamlined so that employees are not limited by artificial boundaries. They should encourage contact, information flow, local responsibility, and especially collaboration among everyone in the organization.

For more information on learning organizations, see *Info-line* No. 9206, "16 Steps to Becoming a Learning Organization."

Systems Thinking

Systems thinking encourages a holistic view—where specific situations are considered in the context of the larger whole. It looks below events to the patterns and structures that created them—just like chaos and complexity theory. The model for systems thinking promoted by Peter Senge, director of the Center for Organizational Learning at MIT's Sloan School of Management, and others usually involves developing graphs of what happens in an organization. In this model, you can characterize recurring feedback loops as system archetypes, generic configurations that fit many situations.

Including perspectives of chaos and complexity theory in systems thinking reveals the limitations of our models. Many graphic representations of systems make them seem simple, linear, and predictable. Yet human systems are relentlessly nonlinear. The challenge is finding their connections, patterns, and underlying order. For more information on systems thinking, see *Info-line* No. 9703, "Systems Thinking."

Pros and Cons

Using chaos and complexity to understand your organization has advantages despite its similarity to the management practices of learning organizations and systems thinking and its relative newness in organizational development. And, as with any new organizational theory, chaos and complexity has attracted its share of criticism.

Pros

■ *Flexibility*

By defining, in broad terms, where you want your organization to go or what you want to accomplish and then allowing employees to discover the best ways to get there, you create a culture that allows your organization to adapt quickly to change. Rather than imposing a process from above that is difficult to change, you allow employees to make choices as changes occur. This allows them to continue working toward the overall goal with a minimum of disruption.

■ *Creativity*

While managers may have more experience in their particular business than the employees, people are naturally creative. Surprising ideas can come from anyone. When you allow employees to design their own course of action, each person's unique life experiences can shape and improve a process in ways that management could never conceive. In addition, employees who shape their own processes are more motivated because their involvement fosters a sense of ownership in the organization's mission.

■ *Stability*

While it may seem odd to list stability as a quality of complex systems, they are actually quite stable due to the interconnectedness of their parts. A large system made up of smaller parts is more stable than a single, large system because of the many checks and balances that exist among the various parts.

Chaos Pioneers

New views of chaos have, as one might imagine, complex beginnings. They emerged from parallel tracks in theoretical physics, mathematics, biology, and meteorology. The following individuals made significant contributions to chaos and complexity theory:

■ **Henri Poincare,** Mathematician
Poincare was one of the first to understand the possibilities of chaos and complexity theory. He noted that effects we often attribute to chance are caused by small or remote causes.

■ **Edward Lorenz,** Meteorologist
Lorenz recognized that long range weather forecasting is impossible because a very small change at the starting point can produce dramatically different outcomes. He coined the term "butterfly effect" to describe *sensitive dependence on initial conditions*—which suggest that something as seemingly inconsequential as a butterfly flapping its wings can affect the weather in a distant area.

■ **Robert May,** Biologist
May, while examining the fluctuations in fish populations, observed that there is a point where increasing bifurcation points (that is, critical points of instability) produce deterministic chaos.

■ **Benoit Mandelbrot,** Mathematician
Mandelbrot developed fractal geometry. Here, an equation is iterated (that is, a factor is multiplied by itself) and produces a complex graphic image with repeated patterns at different scales.

■ **Ilya Prigogine,** Physical Chemist
Prigogine developed the concept of dissipative structures: systems that change form in order to grow and survive. These structures show that disequilibrium and chaos can be the source of order.

■ **David Bohm,** Physicist
Bohm suggested that the universe is a "flowing wholeness" with an implicit order where the whole is contained in each part.

An example of this is the democratic system of government. Even though different political parties are often elected, changing some aspects of the government, the *system* remains fundamentally the same. The same holds true for an organization. When an individual leaves the organization—even at the highest level—his or her replacement brings new ideas. This individual may not do the job exactly the same way, but the organization as a whole does not deviate from its progress toward its vision, its overall goal.

When systems do change, they tend to do so rapidly and often quite drastically once they reach the bifurcation point (that is, the moment of change), and chaos briefly rules. Often, this leads to positive changes as the system adapts to the new environment that has forced it to change.

■ *Leverage*

Systems thinking shows that change can be surprisingly easy if you can identify the right connections. You can leverage a small effort to cause enormous results that would make no sense if you only looked at the results in terms of cause and effect. The key is to find connections between the parts you want to change and alter them in ways that will bring them in line with your objective.

For example, if two people in a group do excellent work on their own or with others but constantly fight when working with each other, the straightforward way to change the system is to prevent them from working with each other. Simple, right? The results, however, may not be limited to just those two people or even to just their work group.

Change in complex systems is never simple: Changes to even a small part of the system can reverberate throughout the system, causing unforeseen—and possibly unpleasant—changes (*remember:* sensitive dependence to initial conditions). Those two people may be more productive working together or may continue fighting even if placed on different teams—spreading the effect to other parts of the organization. Studying and understanding the entire system, therefore, is essential before instituting small changes.

Cons

■ *It's Too New*

Some worry that chaos and complexity is just another entry in a long line of management fads that have entered and stirred up the workplace—often with little or no improvement to show for the efforts of employees and managers. Others see it as nothing more than a new take on systems thinking. Naturally, these battle-scarred veterans of previous management theories will be wary of chaos and complexity until it has proven itself with well-known and respected organizations.

■ *It's Too Soon*

Many theorists and academics question whether chaos and complexity theory is ready to be applied to social systems such as work organizations. They call, not surprisingly, for more study and scholarly discussion before subjecting organizations to the rigors of another management theory. The divergent view is that the only way to further develop and prove that chaos and complexity theory is valid and beneficial is to apply it to actual organizations.

■ *It's Too Simple*

While many scientists and mathematicians feel that chaos and complexity cannot be explained accurately in simple, non-technical terms, people with limited exposure to these disciplines can grasp the fundamentals as they relate to organizations. While there can be a danger to over-simplify the concepts (which take time, effort, and a solid background in math and physics to understand completely), a simplified version allows individuals to determine if chaos and complexity theory would benefit their organization. They can then make an informed decision as to whether or not to delve into it fully.

■ *It's Too Complex*

The study of complex systems has evolved from a number of disciplines (for example, physics, math, biology, and computer science) and there is no single comprehensive theory that covers all of its principles. In addition, much of what has been written is highly technical and inaccessible to those without a solid background in the sciences, including most people with an interest in applying it to organizations. Confusion is bound to result when a theory about understanding and creating *order* and *simplified* structures is called *chaos* and *complexity*.

Training Strategies

The following examples of training strategies can help you explain chaos and complexity.

Frames and Analogies (ways of finding and identifying key concepts in chaos and complexity)	• A cup of coffee can remind us of the importance of the whole rather than the parts. Ingesting the carbon, hydrogen, oxygen, and nitrogen atoms that together make caffeine is not the same as drinking a cup of espresso.
	• A child's kaleidoscope has colored pebbles as the parts of its system. When you turn the toy, the parts shift around as they form and reform the whole. It looks different each time but the same pattern periodically pops up.
	• Watch a pot of water as it is slowly heated. The smooth surface starts to show movement. Small bubbles drift up from the bottom. When the water boils, suddenly the system is in the deep chaos of turbulence. It experiences a phase transition as it makes the change to steam.
	• The final outcome of organizational changes cannot be predicted. Change in complex systems is like a throw of the dice. We do not know exactly what numbers will come up. Each throw is new. We do know, however, that it will not be less than 2 or more than 12.
Everyday Examples (on-the-job illustrations of how employees can see chaos and complexity in their daily activities)	• To understand that the whole is more than the parts, take one department of the organization (for example, payroll, purchasing, or human resources). Does it convey everything the system is and does?
	• Patterns can be seen throughout the system by comparing the corporate mission statement and core values with actual behavior at different levels in the organization. What patterns—similarities and differences—emerge?
	• Just because something worked six months ago does not mean it will have the same result today. Complex systems are filled with complex human beings. The same survey given to the same employees will produce different results each time it is administered.
Exercises and Tools (structured learning activities and aids to promote comprehension and application)	• Find or make a mobile with human figures—the larger and more complicated the better. It shows how a small touch on one point in the system ripples throughout. It also displays the intricate connections between all elements.
	• Ask, "If I tug *this* figure, what specific movement will happen *here*?" We cannot tell exactly what will happen, but we can make a pretty good guess that the second figure will not jump off the string and run away. Behavior in systems will remain within certain bounds.
	• Take a recent organizational change that focused on one or two specific departments or work teams. Trace how it directly and indirectly affected members of other parts of the organization.
	• Consider a recurring problem in a work group. Ask, *"Why does this occur?"* Don't stop with that one simple cause. Ask, *"Why else?"* Keep searching until at least five more "whys" have been identified. Remember, in complex systems, cause and effect is never simple. When we stop with the first and most obvious answer, we rarely uncover the multiple underlying issues that need to be addressed to solve the problem.

Many, most notably Margaret Wheatley, management consultant and author of *Leadership and the New Science* and *A Simpler Way,* suggest that members of organizations should be allowed to form their own self-directed systems with only a few guidelines or rules imposed by management as part of a broad vision of where the organization is headed.

One roadblock to implementing programs such as these, however, has been the highly technical nature of most of the material published on chaos and complexity. Also, managers and employees alike are weary after years of trying to understand the latest buzzwords and adapt to the latest management fads. While these concerns are certainly valid—who has the time or energy for *another* management system, and a confusing one at that—chaos and complexity is so different from previous models that it is worth considering.

While it is always risky to see any new management theory as "The Answer," chaos and complexity theory can give managers a better sense of how their organization works as a whole. This increased understanding could help them become more effective leaders of change.

Implications for Trainers

What prevails over this battle between the pros and cons is the new view of organizational learning that complexity theory brings to the science of management. It focuses attention on the interactive nature of the training and learning process and emphasizes that training cannot be a one-way flow of information from trainers with knowledge to trainees who merely soak up this information. Learners are not passive; they gain knowledge through a two-way interaction with the instructor as well as through interactions with the rest of the class.

Training departments, like other organizations, must develop a broad overall vision of what they want to achieve through training. Individual trainers must be given the freedom to adapt class topics and structures to meet the needs of the organization as well as the individual needs of the trainees. In each class, the trainer will also need to be prepared to adapt to changes in learners' needs as they learn more about the subject being presented.

Organizations love to create detailed charts and diagrams to describe organizational structure and work processes. The resulting layers of boxes and arrows produce static images that reinforce emphasis on isolated components. A common task today is for trainers and consultants to facilitate systems thinking in managers, supervisors, and employees. This means finding ways for system members to "step out of the box."

To do this, trainers are faced with the challenge of helping others achieve the following tasks:

● Set aside old, comfortable ways of viewing organizational life.

● Grasp very abstract concepts and apply them on the job.

● Translate new ways of seeing into behavioral changes.

An understanding of the concepts of chaos and complexity theory can be useful in the change process for many organizations. The study of complex systems takes system thinking to the next level. Unfortunately, it is easy to lose the principles in esoteric discussions about chaos and complexity theory. Individuals with little background in math and physics may prematurely concede defeat in the struggle to comprehend what all the experts are talking about.

Trainers can be helpful in the "translation process." They can provide tools for understanding, so the concepts can be used rather than just admired. Groundbreaking books like Senge's *The Learning Organization* and Wheatley's *Leadership and the New Science* can help trainers and others in the organization move in the right direction.

References & Resources

Articles

Bailyn, Lotte. "Patterned Chaos in Human Resource Management." *Sloan Management Review,* vol. 34, no. 7 1993, pp. 77-83.

Durrance, Bonnie. "The Evolutionary Vision of Dee Hock." *Training & Development,* April 1997, pp. 24-31.

Levy, D. "Chaos Theory and Strategy: Theory, Application, and Managerial Implications." *Strategic Management Journal,* vol. 15, Summer 1994, pp. 167-178.

Michaels, Mark D. "The Chaos Paradigm." *Organization Development Journal,* vol. 7, no. 2 1989, pp. 31-35.

Roos, Johan. "The Poised Organization: Navigating Effectively on Knowledge Landscapes." The Strategy & Complexity Seminar London School of Economics. London, February 12, 1997.

Stamps, David. "The Self-Organizing System." *Training,* April 1997, pp. 30-36.

Stroh, Peter, and Wynne Miller. "Learning to Thrive on Paradox." *Training & Development,* vol. 48, no. 9 1994, pp. 28-39.

Books

Casti, John L. *Complexification: Explaining a Paradoxical World Through the Science of Surprise.* New York: HaperCollins, 1994.

Cohen, Jack, and Ian Stewart. *The Collapse of Chaos: Discovering Simplicity in a Complex World.* New York: Penguin Books, 1994.

Heylighen, Francis. "The Growth of Structural and Functional Complexity During Evolution." Heylighen and D. Aerts (eds.) *The Evolution of Complexity.* Kluwer Academic Publishers, 1997.

Holland, John H. *Hidden Order: How Adaptation Builds Complexity.* Reading, MA: Addison-Wesley, 1995.

Kauffman, Stuart A. *At Home in the Universe.* Oxford University Press, 1995.

———. *The Origins of Order: Self-Organization and Selection in Evolution.* Oxford University Press, 1993.

Lewin, Roger. *Complexity: Life at the Edge of Chaos.* New York: Macmillan, 1992.

Prigogine, Ilya, and Isabelle Stengers. *Order Out of Chaos: Man's New Dialogue with Nature.* New York: Bantam Books, 1984.

Senge, Peter. *The Fifth Discipline: The Art and Practice of the Learning Organization.* New York: Doubleday, 1990.

Stacey, Ralph D. *Managing the Unknowable: Strategic Boundaries Between Order and Chaos in Organizations.* San Francisco: Jossey-Bass, 1992.

Waldrop, M. Mitchell. *Complexity: The Emerging Science at the Edge of Order and Chaos.* New York: Simon & Schuster, 1992.

Wheatley, Margaret. *Leadership and the New Science.* San Francisco: Berrett-Koehler, 1994.

———, and Myron Kellner-Rogers. *A Simpler Way.* San Francisco: Berrett-Koehler, 1996.

Info-lines

"16 Steps to Becoming a Learning Organization." No. 9206.

"Systems Thinking." No. 9703.

Internet Sites

Chaos Think Site
www.orgmind.com/chaos

Santa Fe Institute
www.santafe.edu.

"What is Complexity"
http://pespmc1.vub.ac.be/COMPLEXI.html

Job Aid

Searching for Chaos and Complexity

To be an effective change agent in complex systems, you must have as accurate and complete a picture as possible. Increase the validity of your assessment by gathering information from a number of sources:

- Interview individual staff members.

- Facilitate discussions with small groups of employees.

- Observe daily interactions, the work process, and formal get-togethers (such as, team and staff meetings).

- Identify key informants—representatives from every level of the organization who are knowledgeable and perceptive about tasks, relationships, process, and history.

- Return to these individuals continually to confirm or challenge your interpretations about the workings of the system.

Seek answers to the following questions to help you discover your system's unique signs of chaos and complexity.

I. Wholeness

☐ How is this part connected to the whole?

_____

_____

☐ How is the organizational system connected to external systems?

_____

_____

☐ How effective is collaboration between the parts?

_____

_____

☐ How much competition exists between the parts?

_____

_____

☐ What level of awareness exists in system members of the interconnections?

_____

_____

☐ How prevalent is systems thinking at different levels of the organization?

_____

_____

II. Patterns

☐ What are the formal statements of mission, purpose, and core values?

_____

_____

☐ What evidence of mission, purpose, and values do you see in daily behavior?

_____

_____

☐ What is the extent of alignment between formal policies and actual practices?

_____

_____

☐ What issues or problems continually reoccur?

_____

_____

III. Change

☐ What was a critical turning point in the organization?

_____

_____

☐ What factors led to the bifurcation point?

_____

_____

☐ What alternatives were considered?

_____

_____

☐ Who and what influenced the choice of path?

_____

_____

☐ What were the responses to the change?

_____

_____

☐ What effects linger today?

_____

_____

Job Aid

IV. Parameters

☐ What has been tried that failed miserably?

_____

_____

☐ What change would never be accepted?

_____

_____

☐ What norms—tacit standards and expectations for behavior—exist at different levels and for different organizational members?

_____

_____

V. Puzzles

☐ What have you observed that surprised you?

_____

_____

☐ What makes no sense?

_____

_____

☐ What explanations do members give for system surprises and oddities?

_____

_____

☐ What have you missed by looking at what you did?

_____

_____

Collections

Info-line's Collections offer a highly focused way to get up-to-speed on a particular training discipline. Each is specially grouped for intensive learning.

The Info-line Guide to Training Evaluation

You'll find everything you need to know about training evaluation summed up in manageable morsels. Each issue in this collection focuses on a specific element involved with training evaluation, allowing you to build your skill level from a basic understanding of evaluation to an exact expectation. Starting with the fundamentals, you'll make your way through all the levels of evaluation, including return-on-investment, how to collect data, and conduct testing to achieve those all important learning results.

This one-stop reference source covers:

* Essentials for Evaluation
* Level 1 Evaluation: Reaction and Planned Action
* Level 2 Evaluation: Measuring Learning
* Level 3 Evaluation: Application
* Level 4 Evaluation: Business Results
* Level 5 Evaluation: ROI
* Evaluating Technical Training
* How to Collect Data
* Testing for Learning Outcomes
* Surveys from Start to Finish

ORDER: ILEV. 200 PAGES. LIST PRICE: $75.00.
ASTD MEMBER PRICE: $60.00.

The 1998 Info-line Annual

All 12 subscription issues from 1998 are hard bound together for easy reference in a single volume. Inside each issue is 16-20 pages of easy-to-read facts, graphics, case studies, and job aids—all designed to help you master a subject quickly and put your new knowledge to work immediately. Topics include the following:

* Benchmarking
* Intranets
* The Role of the Performance Evaluator
* The Transfer of Skills Training
* Level 5 Evaluation: ROI
* EPSS and Your Organization
* Chaos and Complexity Theory
* Task Analysis
* Scenario Planning
* Job-Oriented Computer Training
* Fundamentals of HPI
* Selecting a Coach

ORDER CODE: ILA2. 220 PAGES. LIST PRICE: $109.00.
ASTD MEMBER PRICE: $89.00.

The 1997 Info-line Annual

Topics include: • Delivering Quick-Response IBT/CBT Training • From Training to Performance Consulting • Systems Thinking • Action Learning • Essentials for Evaluation • Basics of ISD • High Performance Training Manuals • On-the-Job Training • Evaluating Technical Training: A Functional Approach • Managing the Strategic Planning Process • Effective Job Aids • Instructional Objectives

ORDER CODE: ILA1. 220 PAGES. LIST PRICE: $109.00.
ASTD MEMBER PRICE: $89.00.

To order these and other *Info-line* titles, call us at 1.800.628.2783 or 703.683.8100 and use priority code RXA to expedite your purchase.